BUSINESS ISSUES, COMPETITION AND ENTREPRENEURSHIP

MINIMUM WAGES

OVERVIEW OF STATE PROVISIONS AND FEDERAL POLICY

BUSINESS ISSUES, COMPETITION AND ENTREPRENEURSHIP

Additional books in this series can be found on Nova's website under the Series tab.

Additional e-books in this series can be found on Nova's website under the e-book tab.

BUSINESS ISSUES, COMPETITION AND ENTREPRENEURSHIP

MINIMUM WAGES

OVERVIEW OF STATE PROVISIONS AND FEDERAL POLICY

VIVIAN HAYWOOD
EDITOR

nova publishers
New York

Additional color graphics may be available in the e-book version of this book.

Library of Congress Cataloging-in-Publication Data

ISBN: 978-1-63482-122-3

Published by Nova Science Publishers, Inc. † New York

CONTENTS

PREFACE

This book begins with a discussion of FLSA minimum wage coverage. It provides a summary of state minimum wage laws; and an examination of rates and mechanisms of adjustments in states with minimum wage levels above the FLSA rate.

Chapter 1 – The Fair Labor Standards Act (FLSA), enacted in 1938, is the federal legislation that establishes the general minimum wage that must be paid to all covered workers. While the FLSA mandates broad minimum wage coverage, states have the option of establishing minimum wage rates that are different from those set in it. Under the provisions of the FLSA, an individual is generally covered by the higher of the state or federal minimum wage.

As of January 1, 2015, 29 states and the District of Columbia will have minimum wage rates above the federal rate of $7.25 per hour, with rates ranging from $0.25 to $2.25 above the federal rate. Two states will have minimum wage rates below the federal rate and five states have no state minimum wage requirement. The remaining 14 states have minimum wage rates equal to the federal rate.

In any given year, the exact number of states with a minimum wage rate above the federal rate may vary, depending on the interaction between the federal rate and the mechanisms in place to adjust the state minimum wage. Adjusting minimum wage rates is typically done in one of two ways: (1) 10 states have legislatively scheduled rate increases that may include one or several increments; (2) 11 states use a measure of inflation to index the value of the minimum wage to the general change in prices. In addition to the 11 states currently using an inflation adjustment, four states and DC have chosen a hybrid approach that provides a series of scheduled rate increases, followed by inflation indexation for future minimum wage changes. Thus, a total of 15 states and DC currently, or will in a future year, index state minimum wage rates to a measure of inflation. The remaining 25 states, some of which have minimum wage rates above the federal rate, do not have an adjustment mechanism in place.

Because the federal and state minimum wage rates change at various times and in various increments, the share of the labor force for which the federal rate is the binding wage floor has changed over time. Since 1981, there have been three series of increases in the federal minimum wage rate—1990-1991, 1996-1997, and 2007-2009. During that same period, there have been numerous changes in state minimum wage policies. As a result of those interactions, the share of the U.S. civilian labor force for which the federal minimum wage is the floor has fluctuated but generally declined, and is about 39% as of the beginning of 2015.

Chapter 2 – The Fair Labor Standards Act (FLSA), enacted in 1938, is the federal legislation that establishes the minimum hourly wage that must be paid to all covered workers. The minimum wage provisions of the FLSA have been amended numerous times since 1938, typically for the purpose of expanding coverage or raising the wage rate. Since its establishment, the minimum wage rate has been raised 22 separate times. The most recent change was enacted in 2007 (P.L. 110-28), which increased the minimum wage to its current level of $7.25 per hour.

In addition to setting the federal minimum wage rate, the FLSA provides for several exemptions and subminimum wage categories for certain classes of workers and types of work. Even with these exemptions, the FLSA minimum wage provisions still cover the vast majority of the workforce. Despite this broad coverage, however, the minimum wage directly affects a relatively small portion of the workforce. Currently, there are approximately 3.6 million workers, or 4.7% of all hourly paid workers, whose wages are at or below the federal minimum wage of $7.25 per hour. Approximately three-quarters of minimum wage workers are age 20 or older and nearly two-thirds work part time.

Proponents of increasing the federal minimum wage argue that it may increase earnings for lower income workers, lead to reduced turnover, and increase aggregate demand by providing greater purchasing power for workers receiving a pay increase. Opponents of increasing the federal minimum wage argue that it may result in reduced employment or reduced hours, lead to a general price increase, and reduce profits of firms paying a higher minimum wage.

Chapter 3 – The Fair Labor Standards Act (FLSA) provides workers with minimum wage, overtime pay, and child labor protections. The FLSA covers most, but not all, private and public sector employees. In addition, certain employers and employees are exempt from coverage.

Provisions of the FLSA that are of current interest to Congress include the basic minimum wage, subminimum wage rates, exemptions from overtime and the minimum wage for certain persons who provide companionship services, the exemption for certain employees in computer-related occupations, compensatory time ("comp time") in lieu of overtime pay, and break time for nursing mothers.

In: Minimum Wages
Editor: Vivian Haywood
ISBN: 978-1-63482-122-3

Chapter 1

STATE MINIMUM WAGES: AN OVERVIEW*

David H. Bradley

SUMMARY

The Fair Labor Standards Act (FLSA), enacted in 1938, is the federal legislation that establishes the general minimum wage that must be paid to all covered workers. While the FLSA mandates broad minimum wage coverage, states have the option of establishing minimum wage rates that are different from those set in it. Under the provisions of the FLSA, an individual is generally covered by the higher of the state or federal minimum wage.

As of January 1, 2015, 29 states and the District of Columbia will have minimum wage rates above the federal rate of $7.25 per hour, with rates ranging from $0.25 to $2.25 above the federal rate. Two states will have minimum wage rates below the federal rate and five states have no state minimum wage requirement. The remaining 14 states have minimum wage rates equal to the federal rate.

In any given year, the exact number of states with a minimum wage rate above the federal rate may vary, depending on the interaction between the federal rate and the mechanisms in place to adjust the state minimum wage. Adjusting minimum wage rates is typically done in one of two ways: (1) 10 states have legislatively scheduled rate increases that may include one or several increments; (2) 11 states use a measure of inflation to index the value of the minimum wage to the general change in

* This is an edited, reformatted and augmented version of a Congressional Research Service publication, No. R43792, dated November 18, 2014.

prices. In addition to the 11 states currently using an inflation adjustment, four states and DC have chosen a hybrid approach that provides a series of scheduled rate increases, followed by inflation indexation for future minimum wage changes. Thus, a total of 15 states and DC currently, or will in a future year, index state minimum wage rates to a measure of inflation. The remaining 25 states, some of which have minimum wage rates above the federal rate, do not have an adjustment mechanism in place.

Because the federal and state minimum wage rates change at various times and in various increments, the share of the labor force for which the federal rate is the binding wage floor has changed over time. Since 1981, there have been three series of increases in the federal minimum wage rate—1990-1991, 1996-1997, and 2007-2009. During that same period, there have been numerous changes in state minimum wage policies. As a result of those interactions, the share of the U.S. civilian labor force for which the federal minimum wage is the floor has fluctuated but generally declined, and is about 39% as of the beginning of 2015.

INTRODUCTION

The Fair Labor Standards Act (FLSA), enacted in 1938, is the federal legislation that establishes the general minimum wage that must be paid to all covered workers.[1] The FLSA mandates broad minimum wage coverage. It also specifies certain categories of workers who are not covered by general FLSA wage standards, such as workers with disabilities or certain youth workers.

In 1938, the FLSA established a minimum wage of $0.25 per hour. The minimum wage provisions of the FLSA have been amended numerous times since then, typically to expand coverage or raise the wage rate. Since its establishment, the minimum wage rate has been raised 22 separate times.[2] The most recent change was enacted through P.L. 110-28 in 2007, which increased the minimum wage from $5.15 per hour to its current rate of $7.25 per hour in three steps (the final step occurring in 2009).

States generally have three options in setting their minimum wage policies (1) they can set their own minimum wage provisions that differ from those in the FLSA, (2) they can explicitly tie their minimum wage provisions to the FLSA, or (3) they can include no specific minimum wage provisions in state law.

This report begins with a brief discussion of FLSA minimum wage coverage. It then provides a summary of state minimum wage laws, followed by an examination of rates and mechanisms of adjustments in states with minimum wage levels above the FLSA rate (**Table 1** provides summary data). Next, the report discusses the interaction of federal and state minimum wages over time, and finally, the **Appendix** provides detailed information on the major components of minimum wage policies in all 50 states and DC).

It is important to note that the state policies covered in this report include currently effective policies and policies enacted with an effective date on or before January 1, 2015. Several states enacted legislation in 2014 with an effective date by the beginning of 2015. As such, the description and analysis in the report reflects the effects of legislative and ballot outcomes in 2014.

FLSA Minimum Wage Coverage

The FLSA extends two types of minimum wage coverage to individuals: "enterprise coverage" and "individual coverage."[3] An individual is covered if they meet the criteria for either category.

Enterprise Coverage

To be covered by the FLSA at the enterprise or business level, an enterprise must have at least two employees and annual sales or "business done" of at least $500,000. Annual sales or business done includes all business activities that can be measured in dollars. Thus, for example, retailers are covered by the FLSA if their annual sales are at least $500,000.[4] In non-sales cases, a measure other than sales must be used to determine business done. For example, for enterprises engaged in leasing property, gross amounts paid by tenants for property rental will be considered business done for purposes of determining enterprise coverage.

In addition, regardless of the dollar volume of business, the FLSA applies to hospitals or other institutions primarily providing medical or nursing care for residents; schools (preschool through institutions of higher education); and federal, state, and local governments.

Thus, regardless of how enterprise coverage is determined (by business done or by specified institutional type), all employees of a covered enterprise are considered to be covered by the FLSA.

Individual Coverage

Although an enterprise may not be subject to minimum wage requirements if it has less than $500,000 in annual sales or business done, employees of the enterprise may be covered if they are individually engaged in interstate commerce or in the production of goods for interstate commerce. To be engaged in interstate commerce—the definition of which is fairly broad—employees must produce goods (or have indirect input to the production of those goods) that will be shipped out of the state of production, travel to other states for work, make phone calls or send emails to persons in other states, handle records that are involved in interstate transactions, or provide services to buildings (e.g., janitorial work) in which goods are produced for shipment outside of the state.[5]

While individual coverage is broad under the FLSA, there are also specific exemptions from the federal rate, including individuals with disabilities; youth workers; tipped workers; and executive, administrative, and professional workers, among others.[6]

Minimum Wage Policies in the States

State policymakers may also choose to set labor standards that are different from federal statutes. The FLSA establishes that if a state enacts minimum wage, overtime, or child labor laws more protective of employees than those provided in the FLSA, then state law applies. In the case of minimum wages, this means FLSA-covered workers are entitled to the higher state minimum wage in those states with rates above the federal minimum. On the other hand, FLSA-covered workers would receive the FLSA minimum wage in states that have set minimum wages lower than the federal rate. Given the generally broad minimum wage coverage of the FLSA, it is likely that most workers in states with minimum wages below the federal rate are covered by the FLSA rate.

As of January 1, 2015, the range of state minimum wage rates is as follows:

- 29 states and the District of Columbia have enacted minimum wage rates above the federal rate of $7.25 per hour;
- two states have minimum wage rates below the federal rate;
- five states have no state minimum wage requirement; and

- the remaining 14 states have minimum wage rates equal to the federal rate.[7]

In the states with no minimum wage requirements or wages lower than the federal minimum wage, only individuals who are not covered by the FLSA are subject to those lower rates.

The **Appendix** provides detailed information on state minimum wage policy in all 50 states and DC. Specifically, it includes each state's rate; the year and method of enactment; the mechanism, if any, used to adjust the minimum wage; the legislation authorizing the state minimum wage; and the relevant legislative language regarding the rate and mechanism of adjustment.

The remainder of this report focuses on states with minimum wages above the federal rate.

RATES AND MECHANISMS OF ADJUSTMENT

In states with minimum wage rates above the federal rate, variation occurs mainly across two dimensions: the rate and the mechanism of adjustment to the rate. This section (including data in **Table 1**) summarizes these two dimensions for the states with rates currently above the federal minimum. Current rates range from $0.25 to $2.25 above the federal rate, with a majority of these states using some sort of inflation measure to index the state minimum wage.

Rates

In the 29 states and DC with minimum wage rates above the federal rate, as of January 1, 2015, minimum hourly rates will range from $7.50 per hour in Arkansas, Maine, and New Mexico to $9.47 per hour in Washington state and $9.50 in the District of Columbia. Of the states with minimum wage rates above $7.25,

- the most frequently occurring rate is $8.00, which is the minimum wage in four states;
- the plurality of these states (eight) have rates between $8.01 and $8.25 per hour; and

- 11 states and DC have rates at least $1.00 per hour above the federal rate ($8.25 or higher).

Figure 1 shows the geographic and rate dispersion of state minimum wages. In terms of coverage, a majority of the civilian labor force is in states with a minimum wage rate above the federal rate of $7.25. Specifically, the 29 states and DC with minimum wage rates above $7.25 represent about 61% of the total civilian labor force, which means the federal rate is the wage floor in states representing 39% of the labor force.[8]

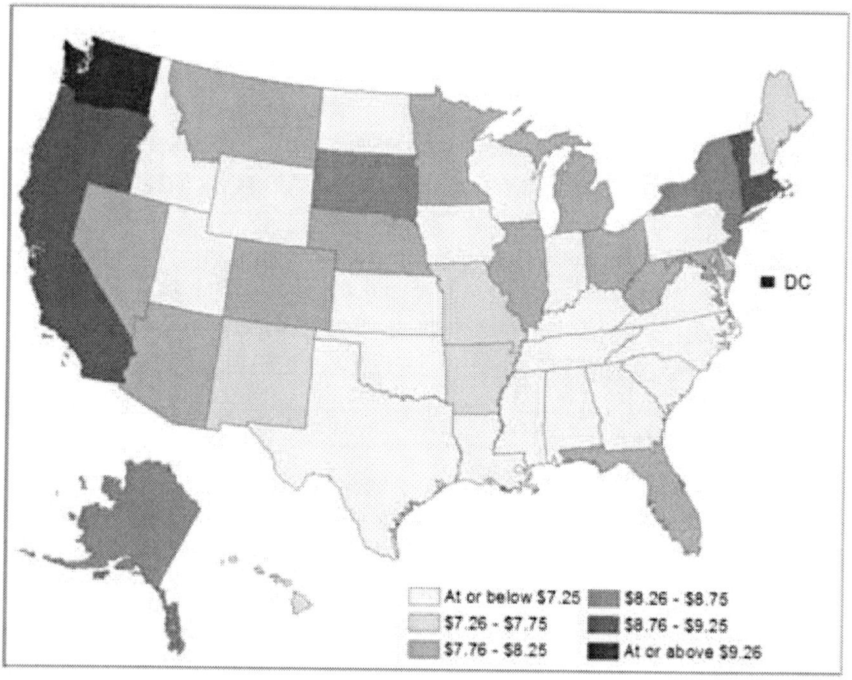

Source: CRS analysis of U.S. Department of Labor data.

Figure 1. State Minimum Wage Rates; As of January 1, 2015.

Mechanisms for Future Adjustments

In any given year, the exact number of states with a minimum wage rate above the federal rate may vary, depending on what mechanism is in place to adjust the state minimum wage.

Some states specifically set rates above the federal rate. Other states have rates above the federal minimum wage because the state minimum wage rate is indexed to a measure of inflation or is increased in legislatively scheduled increments, and thus the state rate changes even if the federal minimum wage stays unchanged.

Below are the two main approaches to regulating the adjustment of state minimum wage rates in states with rates above the federal minimum: legislatively scheduled increases and indexing to inflation.[9] In this section states are counted by the primary method of adjustment. While most states use only one of these methods, some states combine a series of scheduled increases followed by indexing the state rate to a measure of inflation. In these cases, states are counted as "indexing to inflation," as that is the long-term mechanism of adjustment in place.

Legislatively Scheduled Increases

If a state adopts a minimum wage higher than the federal rate, the state legislature may specify a single rate in the enacting legislation and then choose not to address future rates. In these cases, the only mechanism for future rate changes is future legislative action.

Alternatively, a state may specify future rates in legislation through a given date. New York, for example, set a rate of $8.00 per hour in 2014, $8.75 in 2015, and $9.00 in 2016. After the final increase, the rate will remain at $9.00 per hour until further legislative action. This is the same approach taken in the most recent federal minimum wage increase (P.L. 110-28), which increased the minimum wage from $5.15 an hour in 2007 to $7.25 per hour in 2009 in three phases. This mechanism is currently used in 10 states.

Indexing to Inflation

If a minimum wage rate is established as a fixed amount and not increased, its value will erode over time due to inflation. For this reason, several states have attempted to maintain the value of the minimum wage over time by indexing the rate to some measure of inflation. This mechanism provides for automatic changes in the minimum wage over time and does not require legislative action to make annual adjustments.

Of the 11 states currently using an inflation adjustment, six use the Consumer Price Index for All Urban Consumers (CPI-U) and five use the Consumer Price Index for Urban Wage Earners and Clerical Workers (CPI-W).[10]

Four states and DC have chosen a hybrid approach that provides a series of scheduled rate increases, followed by inflation indexation for future minimum wage changes. Specifically, Alaska, Michigan, Vermont, and DC will index the state rate to CPI-U and Minnesota will use a non-CPI measure.[11]

Thus, a total of 15 states and DC currently, or will in a future year, index state minimum wage rates to a measure of inflation.

Reference to the Federal Rate

While scheduled increases and indexation are the two main ways that states adjust their minimum wage rates, a few states also add a reference to the federal minimum wage rate as a possible mechanism of adjustment. Thus any time the federal rate changes, the state rate may change.[12] Currently, Alaska, Connecticut, DC, and Massachusetts use this federal reference to supplement their primary mechanisms of adjusting state minimum wage rates.

- In Alaska, following scheduled increases in 2015 and 2016, the state minimum wage rate will be indexed to the CPI-U for Anchorage. However, the state minimum wage must be at least $1.00 per hour higher than the federal rate. So it is possible that a federal wage increase could trigger an increase in the Alaska minimum wage but the main mechanisms are still the scheduled increases and the indexation to inflation.
- Although Connecticut law includes scheduled rate increases in the minimum wage through 2017, the state rate must exceed the federal minimum wage rate by 0.5% if the federal rate becomes greater than or equal to the state rate.
- Until 2017, DC's minimum wage rate is the higher of the level required by DC statute or the federal rate plus $1.00. Starting in 2017, the DC minimum wage will be indexed to inflation and the reference to the federal rate will no longer be in effect.
- While Massachusetts law includes scheduled rate increases in the minimum wage through 2017, the law also requires that the state rate must be at least $0.50 above federal minimum wage rate.

Table 1. Summary of States with Enacted Minimum Wage Rates Above $7.25 As of January 1, 2015

State	Rate	Adjustment Mechanism	Next Adjustment
Alaska	$8.75	Inflation (Scheduled)	1-1-16 ($9.75)
Arizona	$8.05	Inflation	1-1-16 (CPI-U)
Arkansas	$7.50	Scheduled	1-1-16 ($8.00)
California	$9.00	Scheduled	1-1-16 ($10.00)
Colorado	$8.23	Inflation	1-1-16 (CPI-U)
Connecticut	$9.15	Scheduled (Federal)	1-1-16 ($9.60)
Delaware	$7.75	Scheduled	6-1-15 ($8.25)
District of Columbia	$9.50	Inflation (Scheduled)	7-1-15 ($10.15)
Florida	$8.05	Inflation	1-1-16 (CPI-W)
Hawaii	$7.75	Scheduled	1-1-16 ($8.50)
Illinois	$8.25	None	None
Maine	$7.50	None	None
Maryland	$8.00	Scheduled	7-1-15 ($8.25)
Massachusetts	$9.00	Scheduled (Federal)	1-1-16 ($10.00)
Michigan	$8.15	Inflation (Scheduled)	1-1-16 ($8.50)
Minnesota	$8.00	Inflation (Scheduled)	8-1-15 ($9.00)
Missouri	$7.65	Inflation	1-1-16 (CPI-W)
Montana	$8.05	Inflation	1-1-16 (CPI-U)
Nebraska	$8.00	Scheduled	1-1-16 ($9.00)
Nevada	$8.25	Inflation	7-1-15 (CPI-U)
New Jersey	$8.38	Inflation	1-1-16 (CPI-W)
New Mexico	$7.50	None	None
New York	$8.75	Scheduled	12-31-15 ($9.00)
Ohio	$8.10	Inflation	1-1-16 (CPI-W)
Oregon	$9.25	Inflation	1-1-16 (CPI-U)
Rhode Island	$9.00	None	None
South Dakota	$8.50	Inflation	1-1-16 (CPI-U)
Vermont	$9.15	Inflation (Scheduled)	1-1-16 ($9.60)
Washington	$9.47	Inflation	1-1-16 (CPI-W)
West Virginia	$8.00	Scheduled	1-1-16 ($8.75)

Source: Minimum wage rates are from U.S. Dept. of Labor, http://www.dol.gov/esa/minwage /america.htm; Adjustment mechanisms are from state web sites and National Conference of State Legislatures, http://www.ncsl.org /research/labor-and-employment/state-minimum-wage-chart.aspx.

Notes: In the "Adjustment Mechanism" column, "Inflation" means the state rate is indexed to some measure of inflation, "Scheduled" means that one or more future increases are currently scheduled through existing legislation, and "Federal" means that the state rate is partially set above the federal rate by reference to the federal rate. "Inflation (Scheduled)" means that future increases are currently scheduled and then the state rate becomes indexed to a measure of inflation.

Trends in State Minimum Wages

Because federal and state minimum wages do not change in regular intervals or by regular increments, the number of states and the share of the labor force covered by higher minimum wages changes annually. In general, during periods in which the federal minimum wage remains constant, more states enact higher minimum wages and the share of the workforce for which the federal rate serves as the floor likewise decreases. When the federal rate increases, some state rates become equal to or less than the federal rate.

Table 1 presents a snapshot of minimum wage rates in the 50 states and DC. Of the total civilian labor force, 61% is in states, which as of January 1, 2015, will have minimum wage rates higher than the federal minimum, and 39% is in states in which the federal minimum wage is the wage floor for FLSA-covered workers.

Figure 2 shows the relationship over time between changes in the federal minimum wage rate and changes in the coverage of the federal minimum wage.[13]

Specifically, **Figure 2** plots the nominal and inflation-adjusted value of the federal minimum wage from 1983 to 2015 and the percentage of the civilian labor force residing in states in which the federal wage serves as the floor.[14] If no state had a minimum wage above the federal rate, then the federal minimum wage would be the floor for states in which 100% of the labor force resides; similarly, if every state had a minimum wage above the current rate of $7.25, then the federal rate would not be binding for the labor force. Instead the interaction of federal and state rates has led to the federal minimum wage becoming a fluctuating, but generally decreasing, wage floor for the civilian labor force, particularly during periods in which the federal rate is not increased.

Examining the specific time periods around changes in the federal minimum wage, as shown in **Figure 2**, shows a general trend toward a lower share of the labor force being covered by the federal minimum wage only.

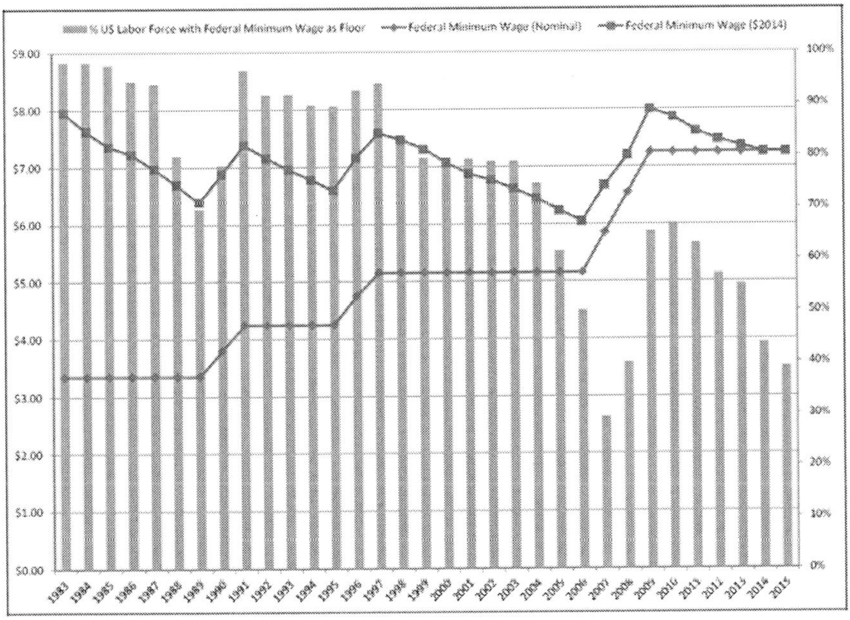

Source: CRS analysis of Tax Policy Center, *State Minimum Wage Rates: 1983-2014*, Washington, DC, http://www.taxpolicycenter.org/taxfacts/displayafact.cfm?Docid=603; US Department of Labor, Wage and Hour Division, *Changes in Basic Minimum Wages in Non-Farm Employment Under State Law: Selected Years 1968-2013*, Washington, DC, http://www.dol.gov/whd/state/stateMinWageHis.htm, and Bureau of Labor Statistics, *Monthly Labor Review*, Washington, DC, multiple years.

Notes: The inflation-adjusted minimum wage is expressed in 2014 dollars based on the Consumer Price Index for All Urban Consumers (CPI-U), U.S. City Average. For 2014, the semi-annual average is used. Prior to 1993, DC did not have a broad minimum wage covering the general population. Thus for periods prior to 1993, this report uses a weighted average of occupation-specific minimum wages, as reported in David Neumark and Olena Nizalova, *Minimum Wage Effects in the Longer Run*, National Bureau of Economic Research, Working Paper 10656, Cambridge, MA, March 2006, http://www.nber.org/papers/w10656. Based on this data, DC has maintained a minimum wage above the federal rate for the entire 1983-2014 period.

Figure 2. The Share of the U.S. Labor Force Residing in States in Which the Federal Minimum Wage is Higher Than the State Minimum Wage.

Federal rate increases in 2007 through 2009 mitigated for a period this reduction, as did earlier changes in the federal rate.

- In the period from 1983 through 1989, the federal minimum wage remained constant at $3.35 per hour. Prior to the federal increases in 1990 and 1991, the number of states with higher minimum wages rose from 3 in 1984 to 16 in 1989 and the share of the U.S. civilian labor force in states for which the federal rate was the floor fell from 98% to 70%.
- Following a two-step federal increase in 1990 and 1991 from $3.35 to $4.25 per hour, the number of states with higher minimum wages fell to 8 in 1992, which meant that the federal rate was the floor for states comprising 92% of the civilian labor force.
- The next federal minimum wage increase occurred in two steps in 1996 and 1997, increasing from $4.25 to $5.15 per hour. Prior to that increase, in 1995, there were 10 states, representing 10% of the civilian labor force, with minimum wages above the federal rate. Immediately following the second increase in 1997, the number of states with higher minimum wages dropped to 8, but the share of the labor force in states for which the federal rate served as a floor decreased to 82%.
- The federal minimum wage did not increase after 1997 until 2007. During much of that period the number of states with higher minimum wages stayed somewhat steady, increasing from 8 (comprising 18% of the civilian labor force) in 1998 to 12 (comprising 21% of the civilian labor force) in 2003. However, by 2006, 22 states representing 50% of the civilian labor force had minimum wage rates above the federal rate. This increase was due in part to a few populous states, such as Florida, Michigan, and New York, adopting minimum wage rates above the federal rate in this period.
- Following the three-step increase in the federal minimum wage from $5.15 to the current $7.25 (2007-2009), 15 states, comprising 33% of the civilian labor force, had rates above the federal minimum wage in 2010. By 2015, this rises to 29 states and DC, which means that the federal rate will be the wage floor in states representing 39% of the civilian labor force.

APPENDIX. SELECTED CHARACTERISTICS OF STATE MINIMUM WAGE POLICIES

For the 29 states and DC with state minimum wage rates above the federal rate by January 1, 2015, Table 1 and much of the text above summarizes information on those states' minimum wage policies, highlighting minimum wage rates and mechanisms used to establish and adjust wage rates. As discussed previously, for those states with current or scheduled minimum wages above the federal rate, three main mechanisms are in place to adjust future rates: (1) scheduled increases, (2) indexation to inflation, or (3) reference to the federal rate plus an add-on (i.e., a state minimum wage is a percentage or dollar amount above the federal rate). For the 21 states with minimum wage rates equal to or below the federal rate, however, there are no mechanisms in place to move rates above the federal rate. Thus, the main difference within this group of states is the relationship of the state rate, if any, to the federal rate.

For those 21 states with minimum wages equal to or below the federal rate, the state rate may be set in four ways:[15]

- No state minimum wage provisions: In five states—Alabama, Louisiana, Mississippi, South Carolina, and Tennessee—there are no provisions for state minimum wage rates. In practice, this means that most workers in these states are covered by the FLSA minimum wage provisions since coverage is generally broad.
- State minimum wage provisions with no reference to the FLSA: Five states have state minimum wage rates but do not reference the FLSA. Two of these states— Georgia and Wyoming—have state rates below $7.25, while three of these states—Kansas, North Dakota, and Wisconsin—have rates equal to $7.25. However, because there is no reference to the FLSA rate or other provision for adjustment in any of these states, the state rate does not change unless the state policy is changed.
- State minimum wage equals the FLSA rate: Six states—Idaho, Indiana, New Hampshire, Oklahoma, Texas, and Virginia—set the state rate equal to the FLSA rate. Thus, when the FLSA rate changes, the state rates in these six states change to equal the FLSA rate.
- State minimum wage equals FLSA rate if FLSA is greater: In four states—Iowa, Kentucky, North Carolina, and Pennsylvania—the state rate is specified separately but includes a provision to equal the FLSA rate if the latter is above the state specified rate.

Table A-1 provides detailed information about minimum wage policies in the 50 states and DC, including those summarized in a more concise manner in Table 1.

Table A-1. Selected State Minimum Wage Policies

State	State Minimum Wage Rate	Year Established / Year Effectivea	Mechanism of Setting State Rate	Mechanism for Future Adjustments	State Legislation or Policy Citation	Pertinent Language and Notes
Alabama	None	n/a	None	None	No state minimum wage law	n/a
Alaska	$8.75	2014 / 2015	State specified rate of $8.75 on January 1, 2015.	Scheduled increases: $9.75 (1-1-16) Beginning January 2017, annual adjustment to be made based on CPI-U for Anchorage Metropolitan Area. In any case, the Alaska minimum wage must be at least $1 above the federal minimum wage.	Alaska Ballot Measure 3 Alaska Statute 23.10.065	Section 3. AS 23.10.065(a) is repealed and reenacted to read: "(a) Except as otherwise provided for in law, an employer shall pay to each employee a minimum wage, as established herein, for hours worked in a pay period, whether the work is measured by time, piece, commission or otherwise. An employer may not apply tips or gratuities bestowed upon employees as a credit toward payment of the minimum hourly wage required by this section. Tip credit as defined by the Fair Labor Standards Act of 1938 as amendment does not apply to the minimum wage established by this section.

State	State Minimum Wage Rate	Year Established / Year Effectivea	Mechanism of Setting State Rate	Mechanism for Future Adjustments	State Legislation or Policy Citation	Pertinent Language and Notes
						Beginning with the passage of this Act, the minimum wage shall be $8.75 per hour effective January 1, 2015, $9.75 per hour effective January 1, 2016 and thereafter adjusted annually for inflation. The adjustment shall be calculated each September 30, for the proceeding January-December calendar year, by the Alaska Department of Labor and Workforce Development, using 100 percent of the rate of inflation based on the Consumer Price Index for all urban consumers for the Anchorage metropolitan area, compiled by the Bureau of Labor Statistics, United States Department of Labor; the department shall round the adjusted minimum hourly wage up to the nearest one cent; the adjusted minimum hourly wage shall apply to work performed beginning on January 1 through December 31 of the year for which it is effective. Section 4.

Table A-1. (Continued)

State	State Minimum Wage Rate	Year Established / Year Effectivea	Mechanism of Setting State Rate	Mechanism for Future Adjustments	State Legislation or Policy Citation	Pertinent Language and Notes
						If the minimum wage determined under Section 3 is less than one dollar over the federal minimum wage, the Alaska minimum wage shall be set at one dollar over the federal minimum wage. This amount shall be adjusted in subsequent years by the method established in Section 3."
Arizona	$8.05	2006 / 2015	State specified rate of $6.75 on January 1, 2007, followed by adjustment on January 1, 2008, and each successive January 1.	Inflation: Indexed to CPI-U, U.S. City Average as of January 1, 2008.	Arizona Revised Statutes, 23-363	"The minimum wage shall be increased on January 1, 2008 and on January 1 of successive years by the increase in the cost of living. The increase in the cost of living shall be measured by the percentage increase as of August of the immediately preceding year over the level as of August of the previous year of the consumer price index (all urban consumers, U.S. city average for all items) or its successor index as published by the U.S. department of labor or its successor agency, with the amount of the minimum wage increase rounded to the nearest multiple of five cents."

State	State Minimum Wage Rate	Year Established / Year Effectivea	Mechanism of Setting State Rate	Mechanism for Future Adjustments	State Legislation or Policy Citation	Pertinent Language and Notes
Arkansas	$7.50	2014 / 2015	State specified rate of $7.50 on January 1, 2015.	Scheduled increases: $8.00 (1-1-16) $8.50 (1-1-17)	Arkansas Code 11-4-210	"Beginning January 1, 2015, every employer shall pay each of his or her employees wages at the rate of not less than seven dollars and fifty cents ($7.50) per hour, beginning January 1, 2016 the rate of not less than eight dollars ($8.00) per hour and beginning January 1, 2017 the rate of not less than eight dollars and fifty cents ($8.50) per hour except as otherwise provided in this subchapter."
California	$9.00	2013 / 2014	State specified rate of $9.00 on July 1, 2014, followed by scheduled increase.	Scheduled increases: $10.00 (1-1-16)	California Labor Code 1182.12	"Notwithstanding any other provision of this part, on and after July 1, 2014, the minimum wage for all industries shall be not less than nine dollars ($9.00) per hour, and on and after January 1, 2016, the minimum wage for all industries shall be not less than ten dollars ($10.00) per hour."
Colorado	$8.23	2006 / 2015	State specified rate of $6.85 on January 1, 2007, followed by adjustment on January 1, 2008, and each successive January 1.	Inflation: Indexed to CPI-U, Denver-Boulder-Greeley Metro Area as of January 1, 2008.	Colorado Constitution, Art. XVIII, Section 15	"Effective January 1, 2007, Colorado's minimum wage shall be increased to $6.85 per hour and shall be adjusted annually for inflation, as measured by the Consumer Price Index used for Colorado."

Table A-1. (Continued)

State	State Minimum Wage Rate	Year Established / Year Effectivea	Mechanism of Setting State Rate	Mechanism for Future Adjustments	State Legislation or Policy Citation	Pertinent Language and Notes
Connecticut	$9.15	2013 / 2015	State specified rate of $8.70 on January 1, 2014, followed by scheduled increases.	Scheduled increases: $9.60 (1-1-16) $10.10 (1-1-17) State rate must exceed federal minimum wage rate by 0.5% if the federal rate becomes greater than or equal to the state rate.	Connecticut State Statutes Section 31-58	"Effective January 1, 2014, not less than eight dollars and seventy cents per hour, and effective January 1, 2015, not less than nine dollars and fifteen cents per hour, and effective January 1, 2016, not less than nine dollars and sixty cents per hour, and effective January 1, 2017, not less than ten dollars and ten cents per hour or one-ha of one per cent rounded to the nearest whole cent more than the highest federal minimum wage, whichever is greater."
Delaware	$7.75	2014 / 2014	State specified rate of $7.75 on June 1, 2014, followed by scheduled increase.	Scheduled increases: $8.25 (6-1-15) State rate must match federal minimum wage rate if the latter is greater.	Delaware Code Title 19-902	"(a) Except as may otherwise be provided under this chapter, every employer shall pay to every employee in any occupation wages of a rate: (1) Not less than $ 7.75 per hour effective June 1, 2014; and (2) Not less than $ 8.25 per hour effective June 1, 2015. Upon the establishment of a federal minimum wage in excess of the state minimum wage,

State	State Minimum Wage Rate	Year Established / Year Effectivea	Mechanism of Setting State Rate	Mechanism for Future Adjustments	State Legislation or Policy Citation	Pertinent Language and Notes
						the minimum wage in this State shall be equal in amount to the federal minimum wage, except as may otherwise be provided under this chapter."
DC	$9.50	2014 / 2014	State specified rate of $9.50 on July 1, 2014, followed by scheduled increases in 2015 and 2016, followed by adjustment on July 1, 2017, and each successive July 1.	Scheduled increases: $10.50 (7-1-15) $11.50 (7-1-16) Indexed to CPI-U, Washington Metro Area as of July 1, 2017. Note: For 2015 and 2016, the minimum wage is the greater of the scheduled increases or the FLSA rate plus $1.	D.C. Code Section 32-1003	"(3) Except as provided in subsection (h) of this section, as of July 1, 2014, the minimum wage required to be paid to any employee by any employer in the District of Columbia shall be $ 9.50 an hour, or the minimum wage set by the United States government pursuant t the Fair Labor Standards Act, plus $1, whichever is greater. (4) Except as provided in subsection (h) of this section, as of July 1, 2015, the minimum wage required to be paid to any employee by any employer in the District of Columbia shall be $ 10.50 an hour, or the minimum wage set by the United States government pursuant to the Fair Labor Standards Act, plus $1, whichever is greater. (5) Except as provided in subsection (h) of this section, as of July 1, 2016,

Table A-1. (Continued)

State	State Minimum Wage Rate	Year Established / Year Effectivea	Mechanism of Setting State Rate	Mechanism for Future Adjustments	State Legislation or Policy Citation	Pertinent Language and Notes
						the minimum wage required to be paid to any employee by any employer in the District of Columbia shall be $11.50 an hour, or the minimum wage set by the United States government pursuant to the Fair Labor Standards Act, plus $1, whichever is greater. (6) (A) Except as provided in subsection (h) of this section, beginning on July 1, 2017 and no later than July 1 of each successive year, the minimum wage provided in this subsection shall be increased in proportion to the annual average increase, if any, in the Consumer Price Index for All Urban Consumers in the Washington Metropolitan Statistical Area published by the Bureau of Labor Statistics of the United States Department of Labor for the previous calendar year. Any increase under this paragraph shall be adjusted to the nearest multiple of $.05."

State	State Minimum Wage Rate	Year Established / Year Effective[a]	Mechanism of Setting State Rate	Mechanism for Future Adjustments	State Legislation or Policy Citation	Pertinent Language and Notes
Florida[b]	$8.05	2004; 2005 / 2015	State specified rate of $6.15 on May 2, 2005, followed by adjustment on January 1, 2006, and each successive January 1.	Inflation: Indexed to CPI-W, South Region as of January 1, 2006.	Florida Labor Statute 448- 110 (4)(a)	"Beginning September 30, 2005, and annually on September 30 thereafter, the Department of Economic Opportunity shall calculate an adjusted state minimum wage rate by increasing the state minimum wage by the rate of inflation for the 12 months prior to September 1. In calculating the adjusted state minimum wage, the Department of Economic Opportunity shall use the Consumer Price Index for Urban Wage Earners and Clerical Workers, not seasonally adjusted, for the South Region or a successor index as calculated by the United States Department of Labor. Each adjusted state minimum wage rate shall take effect on the following January 1, with the initial adjusted minimum wage rate to take effect on January 1, 2006."

Table A-1. (Continued)

State	State Minimum Wage Rate	Year Established / Year Effectivea	Mechanism of Setting State Rate	Mechanism for Future Adjustments	State Legislation or Policy Citation	Pertinent Language and Notes
Georgia	$5.15	2001 / 2001	State specified rate of $5.15 in 2001,	None	Georgia Code 34-4-3	"(a) Except as otherwise provided in this Code section, every employer, whether a person, firm, or corporation, shall pay to all covered employees a minimum wage which shall be not less than $5.15 per hour for each hour worked in the employment of such employer."
Hawaii	$7.75	2014 / 2015	State specified rate of $7.75 on January 1, 2015.	Scheduled increases: $8.50 (1-1-16) $9.25 (1-1-17) $10.10 (1-1-18)	Hawaii Revised Statutes 387-2	"(a) Except as provided in section 387-9 and this section, every employer shall pay to each employee employed by the employer, wages at the rate of not less than: (1) $6.25 per hour beginning January 1, 2003; (2) $6.75 per hour beginning January 1, 2006; (3) $7.25 per hour beginning January 1, 2007; (4) $7.75 per hour beginning January 1, 2015; (5) $8.50 per hour beginning January 1, 2016; (6) $9.25 per hour beginning January 1, 2017; and (7) $10.10 per hour beginning January 1, 2018." Note:

State	State Minimum Wage Rate	Year Established / Year Effectivea	Mechanism of Setting State Rate	Mechanism for Future Adjustments	State Legislation or Policy Citation	Pertinent Language and Notes
						This is language from legislation signed into law in May 2014, but a 2005 law had already set the state minimum wage at $7.25, effective 1-1-07.
Idaho	$7.25	2007 / 2009	State specified rate of $5.15 on September 1, 1997, thereafter equaling the FLSA rate.	Next FLSA minimum wage rate change.	Idaho Statutes 44-1502	"Except as hereinafter otherwise provided, no employer shall pay to any of his employees any wages computed at a rate of less than four dollars and seventy-five cents ($4.75) commencing April 1, 1997, and five dollars and fifteen cents ($5.15) commencing September 1, 1997, per hour for employment. The amount of the minimum wage shall conform to, and track with, the federal minimum wage."
Illinois	$8.25	2006 / 2010	State specified rate of $8.25 on July 1, 2010.	None	Illinois Compiled Statutes 820-105/4	"On and after July 1, 2010 every employer shall pay to each of his or her employees who is 18 years of age or older in every occupation wages of not less than $8.25 per hour."

Table A-1. (Continued)

State	State Minimum Wage Rate	Year Established / Year Effectivea	Mechanism of Setting State Rate	Mechanism for Future Adjustments	State Legislation or Policy Citation	Pertinent Language and Notes
Indiana	$7.25	2007 / 2009	State specified rate equal to FLSA rate on July 1, 2007, thereafter equaling the FLSA rate.	Next FLSA minimum wage rate change.	Indiana Code 22-2-2-1	"(h) Except as provided in subsections (c) and (j), every employer employing at least two (2) employees during a work week shall, in any work week in which the employer is subject to this chapter, pay each of the employees in any work week beginning on or after June 30, 2007, wages of not less than the minimum wage payable under the federal Fair Labor Standards Act of 1938, as amended (29 U.S.C. 201 et seq.)."
Iowa	$7.25	2007 / 2008	State specified rate of $7.25 on January 1, 2008.	State rate must match federal minimum wage rate if the latter is greater.	Iowa Code 91D.1	"1. a. The state hourly wage shall be at least $6.20 as of April 1, 2007, and $7.25 as of January 1, 2008. b. Every employer, as defined in the federal Fair Labor Standards Act of 1938, as amended to January 1, 2007, shall pay to each of the employer's employees, as defined in the federal Fair Labor Standards Act of 1938, as amended to January 1, 2007, the state hourly wage stated

State	State Minimum Wage Rate	Year Established / Year Effectivea	Mechanism of Setting State Rate	Mechanism for Future Adjustments	State Legislation or Policy Citation	Pertinent Language and Notes
						in paragraph "a", or the current federal minimum wage, pursuant to 29 U.S.C. § 206, as amended, whichever is greater."
Kansas	$7.25	2009 / 2010	State specified rate of $7.25 on January 1, 2010.	None	Kansas Statute 44-1203	"Except as otherwise provided in the minimum wage and maximum hours law, every employer shall pay to each employee wages at a rate as follows: (1) Prior to January 1, 2010, employee wages shall be paid at a rate of not less than $2.65 an hour; and (2) on and after January 1, 2010, employee wages shall be paid at a rate of not less than $7.25 an hour."
Kentucky	$7.25	2007 / 2009	State specified rate of $7.25 on July 1, 2009.	State rate must match federal minimum wage rate if the latter is greater.	Kentucky Revised Code 337.275	"Except as may otherwise be provided by this chapter, every employer shall pay to each of his employees wages at a rate of not less than five dollars and eighty-five cents ($5.85) an hour beginning on June 26, 2007, not less than six dollars and fifty-five cents ($6.55 an hour beginning July 1, 2008, and not less than seven dollars and twenty-five cents ($7.25) an hour beginning July 1, 2009.

Table A-1. (Continued)

State	State Minimum Wage Rate	Year Established / Year Effectivea	Mechanism of Setting State Rate	Mechanism for Future Adjustments	State Legislation or Policy Citation	Pertinent Language and Notes
						If the federal minimum hourly wage as prescribed by 29 U.S.C. sec. 206(a)(1) is increased in excess of the minimum hourly wage in effect under this subsection, the minimum hourly wage under this subsection shall be increased to the same amount, effective on the same date as the federal minimum hourly wage rate."
Louisiana	None	n/a	None	None	No state minimum wage law	
Maine	$7.50	2007 / 2009	State specified rate of $7.50 on October 1, 2009.	State rate must match federal minimum wage rate if the latter is greater, but only up to $1 above the state rate.	Maine Revised Statutes 26, Section 664 (1)	"Starting October 1, 2009, the minimum hourly wage is $7.50 per hour. If the highest federal minimum wage is increased in excess of the minimum wage in effect under this section, the minimum wage under this section is increased to the same amount, effective on the same date as the increase in the federal minimum wage, but in no case may the minimum wage exceed the minimum wage otherwise in effect under this section by more than $1 per hour."

State	State Minimum Wage Rate	Year Established / Year Effectivea	Mechanism of Setting State Rate	Mechanism for Future Adjustments	State Legislation or Policy Citation	Pertinent Language and Notes
Maryland	$8.00	2014 / 2015	State specified rate of $8.00 on January 1, 2015.	Scheduled increases: $8.25 (7-1-15) $8.75 (7-1-16) $9.25 (7-1-17) $10.10 (7-1-18) State rate must match federal minimum wage if the latter is greater.	Maryland Labor and Employment Code 3-413	"(b) In general.—Except as provided in subsection (d) of this section and § 3-414 of this subtitle, each employer shall pay: (1) to each employee who is subject to both the federal Act and this subtitle, at least the greater of: (i) the minimum wage for that employee under the federal Act; or (ii) the State minimum wage rate set under subsection (c) of this section; and (2) each other employee who is subject to this subtitle, at least: (i) the greater of: 1. the highest minimum wage under the federal Act; or 2. the State minimum wage rate set under subsection (c) of this section; or (ii) a training wage under regulations that the Commissioner adopts that include the conditions and limitations authorized under the federal Fair Labor Standards Amendments of 1989. (c) State minimum wage.—

Table A-1. (Continued)

State	State Minimum Wage Rate	Year Established / Year Effectivea	Mechanism of Setting State Rate	Mechanism for Future Adjustments	State Legislation or Policy Citation	Pertinent Language and Notes
						The State minimum wage rate is: (1) for the 6-month period beginning January 1, 2015, $8.00 per hour; (2) for the 12-month period beginning July 1, 2015, $8.25 per hour; (3) for the 12-month period beginning July 1, 2016, $8.75 per hour; (4) for the 12-month period beginning July 1, 2017, $9.25 per hour; and (5) beginning July 1, 2018, $10.10 per hour." Note: This is language from legislation signed into law in May 2014, but a 2005 law had already set the state minimum wage at $7.25, effective 1-1-07.
Massachusetts	$9.00	2014 / 2015	State specified rate of $9.00 on January 1, 2015, subject to a minimum of $0.50 higher than the FLSA rate.	Scheduled increases: $10.00 (1-1-16) $11.00 (1-1-17) State rate must be at least $0.50 above federal minimum wage rate.	Massachusetts General Laws Chapter 151, Section 1	"A wage of less than $9.00 per hour, in any occupation, as defined in this chapter, shall conclusively be presumed to be oppressive and unreasonable ... Notwithstanding the provisions of this section, in no case shall the minimum wage rate be less than $.50 higher than the effective federal minimum rate."

State	State Minimum Wage Rate	Year Established / Year Effectivea	Mechanism of Setting State Rate	Mechanism for Future Adjustments	State Legislation or Policy Citation	Pertinent Language and Notes
Michigan	$8.15	2014 / 2014	State specified rate of $8.15 on September 1, 2014.	Scheduled increases: $8.50 (1-1-16) $8.90 (1-1-17) $9.25 (1-1-18) Beginning January 2019, annual adjustment to be made based on CPI-U for Midwest region. This annual adjustment is limited to 3.5% increase and does not take effect if the state unemployment rate in the prior year was 8.5% or greater.	Michigan Compiled Laws 408.414	"Sec. 4. (1) Subject to the exceptions specified in this act, the minimum hourly wage rate is: (a) Before September 1, 2014, $ 7.40. (b) Beginning September 1, 2014, $ 8.15. (c) Beginning January 1, 2016, $ 8.50. (d) Beginning January 1, 2017, $ 8.90. (e) Beginning January 1, 2018, $ 9.25. (2) Every January beginning in January 2019, the state treasurer shall adjust the minimum wage by an amount determined by the state treasurer at the end of the preceding calendar year to reflect the average annual percentage change in the consumer price index for the most recent 5-year period for which data are available. As used in this subsection, "consumer price index" means the most comprehensive index of consumer prices available for the midwest region from the bureau of labor statistics of the United States department of labor.

Table A-1. (Continued)

State	State Minimum Wage Rate	Year Established / Year Effectivea	Mechanism of Setting State Rate	Mechanism for Future Adjustments	State Legislation or Policy Citation	Pertinent Language and Notes
						The wage and hours division of the department of licensing and regulatory affairs shall post the adjusted minimum wage on its website by February 1 of the year it is calculated, and the adjusted rate is effective beginning April 1 of that year. An annual increase under this subsection shall not exceed 3.5%. (3) An increase in the minimum hourly wage rate as prescribed in subsection (2) does not take effect if the unemployment rate determined by the bureau of labor statistics, United States department of labor, for this state is 8.5% or greater for the year preceding the year of the prescribed increase."
Minnesota	$8.00c	2014 / 2014	State specified rate of $8.00 on August 1, 2014.	Scheduled increases: $9.00 (8-1-15) $9.50 (8-1-16) Beginning 1-1-18, minimum	Minnesota Statutes 177.24	"(1) every large employer must pay each employee wages at a rate of at least: (i) $ 8.00 per hour beginning August 1, 2014; (ii) $ 9.00 per hour beginning August 1, 2015; (iii) $ 9.50 per hour beginning August 1, 2016; and

State	State Minimum Wage Rate	Year Established / Year Effectivea	Mechanism of Setting State Rate	Mechanism for Future Adjustments	State Legislation or Policy Citation	Pertinent Language and Notes
				wage rate will be annually adjusted according to inflation (implicit price deflator), subject to a maximum increase of 2.5%.		(iv) the rate established under paragraph (f) beginning January 1, 2018; (f) No later than August 31 of each year, beginning in 2017, the commissioner shall determine the percentage increase in the rate of inflation, as measured by the implicit price deflator, national data for personal consumption expenditures as determined by the United States Department of Commerce, Bureau of Economic Analysis during the 12-month period immediately preceding that August or, if that data is unavailable, during the most recent 12-month period for which data is available. The minimum wage rates in paragraphs (b), (c), (d), and (e) are increased by the lesser of: (1) 2.5 percent, rounded to the nearest cent; or (2) the percentage calculated by the commissioner, rounded to the nearest cent. A minimum wage rate shall not be reduced under this paragraph. The new minimum wage rates determined under this paragraph take effect on the next January 1."

Table A-1. (Continued)

State	State Minimum Wage Rate	Year Established / Year Effectivea	Mechanism of Setting State Rate	Mechanism for Future Adjustments	State Legislation or Policy Citation	Pertinent Language and Notes
Mississippi	None	n/a	None	None	No state minimum wage law	n/a
Missouri	$7.65	2006 / 2015	State specified rate of $6.50 on January 1, 2007, followed by adjustment on January 1, 2008, and each successive January 1.	Inflation: CPI-W	Missouri Revised Statutes 290.502	"The minimum wage shall be increased or decreased on January 1, 2008, and on January 1 of successive years, by the increase or decrease in the cost of living. On September 30, 2007, and on each September 30 of each successive year, the director shall measure the increase or decrease in the cost of living by the percentage increase or decrease as of the preceding July over the level as of July of the immediately preceding year of the Consumer Price Index for Urban Wage Earners and Clerical Workers (CPI-W) or successor index as published by the U.S. Department of Labor or its successor agency, with the amount of the minimum wage increase or decrease rounded to the nearest five cents."

State	State Minimum Wage Rate	Year Established / Year Effectivea	Mechanism of Setting State Rate	Mechanism for Future Adjustments	State Legislation or Policy Citation	Pertinent Language and Notes
Montana	$8.05	2006 / 2015	State specified rate of higher of $6.15 or FLSA rate, followed by adjustment on January 1, 2007, and each successive January 1.	Inflation: CPI-U, U.S. City Average	Montana Code Annotated 39-3-409	"No later than September 30 of each year, an adjustment of the wage amount specified in subsection (1) must be made based upon the increase, if any, from August of the preceding year to August of the year in which the calculation is made in the consumer price index, U.S. city average, all urban consumers, for all items, as published by the bureau of labor statistics of the United States department of labor."
Nebraska	$8.00	2014 / 2015	State specified rate of $8.00 on January 1, 2015.	Scheduled increases: $9.00 (1-1-16)	Nebraska Revised Statutes 48-1203	"Except as otherwise provided in this section and section 48-1203.01, every employer shall pay to each of his or her employees a minimum wage of: (a) Seven dollars and twenty-five cents per hour through December 31, 2014; (b) Eight dollars per hour on and after January 1, 2015, through December 31, 2015; and (c) Nine dollars per hour on and after January 1, 2016."

Table A-1. (Continued)

State	State Minimum Wage Rate	Year Established / Year Effectivea	Mechanism of Setting State Rate	Mechanism for Future Adjustments	State Legislation or Policy Citation	Pertinent Language and Notes
Nevada	$8.25d	2006 / 2010	State specified rate of $5.15 (or $6.15 with no health insurance) in 2006, followed by adjustment on July 1, 2007, and each successive July 1.	Inflation: CPI-U, U.S. City Average. State rate is the greater of $5.15 ($6.15) plus the cumulative inflation since 12/31/04 (subject to a maximum annual increase of 3%) or the increases in the federal minimum wage over $5.15.	Nevada Constitution Article 15 Sect. 16	"Each employer shall pay a wage to each employee of not less than the hourly rates set forth in this section. The rate shall be five dollars and fifteen cents ($5.15) per hour worked, if the employer provides health benefits as described herein, or six dollars and fifteen cents ($6.15) per hour if the employer does not provide such benefits. Offering health benefits within the meaning of this section shall consist of making health insurance available to the employee for the employee and the employee's dependents at a total cost to the employee for premiums of not more than 10 percent of the employee's gross taxable income from the employer. These rates of wages shall be adjusted by the amount of increases in the federal minimum wage over $5.15 per hour, or, if greater, by the cumulative increase in the cost of living.

State	State Minimum Wage Rate	Year Established / Year Effectivea	Mechanism of Setting State Rate	Mechanism for Future Adjustments	State Legislation or Policy Citation	Pertinent Language and Notes
						The cost of living increase shall be measured by the percentage increase as of December 31 in any year over the level as of December 31, 2004 of the Consumer Price Index (All Urban Consumers, U.S. City Average) as published by the Bureau of Labor Statistics, U.S. Department of Labor or the successor index or federal agency. No CPI adjustment for any one-year period may be greater than 3%."
New Hampshire	$7.25	2007 / 2008	State specified rate equal to FLSA rate on July 1, 2007, thereafter equaling the FLSA rate.	Next FLSA minimum wage rate change.	New Hampshire Revised Statutes 279:21	"Unless otherwise provided by statute, no person, firm, or corporation shall employ any employee at an hourly rate lower than that set forth in the federal minimum wage law, as amended." Note: This is language from the current statute as revised by 2011 legislation, but a 2007 law had already set the state minimum wage at $7.25.

Table A-1. (Continued)

State	State Minimum Wage Rate	Year Established / Year Effectivea	Mechanism of Setting State Rate	Mechanism for Future Adjustments	State Legislation or Policy Citation	Pertinent Language and Notes
New Jersey	$8.38	2013 / 2015	State specified rate of $8.25 on January 1, 2014, followed by adjustment on each successive January 1.	Inflation: CPI-W State rate must match federal minimum wage if the latter is greater.	New Jersey Constitution Article I, paragraph 23	"A wage rate of not less than the rate required by that act, or $8.25 per hour, whichever is more. On the September 30 next following the date of the approval of this amendment, and on September 30 of each subsequent year, the State minimum wage rate shall be increased, effective the following January 1, by any increase during the one year prior to that September 30 in the consumer price index for all urban wage earners and clerical workers (CPI-W) as calculated by the federal government."
New Mexico	$7.50	2007 / 2009	State specified rate of $7.50 on January 1, 2009.	None	New Mexico Statutes 50- 4-22	"An employer shall pay an employee the minimum wage rate of six dollars fifty cents ($ 6.50) an hour. As of January 1, 2009, an employer shall pay the minimum wage rate of seven dollars fifty cents ($7.50) an hour."

State	State Minimum Wage Rate	Year Established / Year Effectivea	Mechanism of Setting State Rate	Mechanism for Future Adjustments	State Legislation or Policy Citation	Pertinent Language and Notes
New York	$8.75	2013 / 2015	State specified rate of $8.75 on December 31, 2014.	Scheduled increases: $9.00 (12-31-15) State rate must match federal minimum wage rate if the latter is greater.	New York Codes, Rules, and Regulations Title 12, Section 141-1.3	"For all employees except janitors in residential buildings, the basic minimum hourly rate shall be: (c) $8.00 per hour on and after December 31, 2013; (d) $8.75 per hour on and after December 31, 2014; (e) $9.00 per hour on and after December 31, 2015, or, if greater, such other wage as may be established by Federal law pursuant to 29 U.S.C. section 206 or its successors."
North Carolina	$7.25	2006 / 2009	State specified rate of higher of $6.15 or FLSA rate.	State rate must match federal minimum wage rate if the latter is greater.	North Carolina General Statutes 95-25.3	"Every employer shall pay to each employee who in any workweek performs any work, wages of at least six dollars and fifteen cents ($6.15) per hour or the minimum wage set forth in paragraph 1 of section 6(a) of the Fair Labor Standards Act, 29 U.S.C. 206(a)(1), as that wage may change from time to time, whichever is higher, except as otherwise provided in this section."

Table A-1. (Continued)

State	State Minimum Wage Rate	Year Established / Year Effectivea	Mechanism of Setting State Rate	Mechanism for Future Adjustments	State Legislation or Policy Citation	Pertinent Language and Notes
North Dakota	$7.25	2007 / 2009	State specified rate of $7.25 on July 24, 2009.	None	North Dakota Code 34-06-22	"Except as otherwise provided under this chapter and rules adopted by the commissioner, every employer shall pay to each of the employer's employees: a. Effective on the effective date of this section, a wage of at least five dollars and eighty-five cents per hour; b. Effective twelve months after the effective date of this section, a wage of at least six dollars and fifty-five cents per hour; and c. Effective twenty-four months after the effective date of this section, a wage of at least seven dollars and twenty-five cents per hour."
Ohio	$8.10	2006 / 2015	State specified rate of $6.85 on January 1, 2007, followed by adjustment on each successive January 1.	Inflation: CPI-W	Ohio Constitution 2.34a	"On the thirtieth day of each September, beginning in 2007, this state minimum wage rate shall be increased effective the first day of the following January by the rate of inflation for the twelve month period prior to that September according to the consumer price index or its successor index for all

State	State Minimum Wage Rate	Year Established / Year Effective[a]	Mechanism of Setting State Rate	Mechanism for Future Adjustments	State Legislation or Policy Citation	Pertinent Language and Notes
						urban wage earners and clerical workers for all items as calculated by the federal government rounded to the nearest five cents."
Oklahoma	$7.25	1983 / 2009	State specified rate equal to FLSA rate on November 1, 1983, thereafter equaling the FLSA rate.	Next FLSA minimum wage rate change.	Oklahoma Statutes 40-197.2	"Except as otherwise provided in the Oklahoma Minimum Wage Act, no employer within the State of Oklahoma shall pay any employee a wage of less than the current federal minimum wage for all hours worked."
Oregon	$9.25	2003 / 2015	State specified rate of $6.90 on January 1, 2003, followed by adjustment on each successive January 1.	Inflation: CPI-U, U.S. City Average	Oregon Revised Statutes 653.025	"No later than September 30 of each year, beginning in calendar year 2003, the commissioner shall calculate an adjustment of the wage amount specified in subsection (1) of this section based upon the increase (if any) from August of the preceding year to August of the year in which the calculation is made in the U.S. City Average Consumer Price Index for All Urban Consumers for All Items as prepared by the Bureau of Labor Statistics of the United States Department of Labor or its successor. (c) The wage amount established under this subsection shall: (A) Be rounded to the nearest five cents."

Table A-1. (Continued)

State	State Minimum Wage Rate	Year Established / Year Effectivea	Mechanism of Setting State Rate	Mechanism for Future Adjustments	State Legislation or Policy Citation	Pertinent Language and Notes
Pennsylvania	$7.25	2006 / 2009	State specified rate of $7.15 on July 1, 2007.	State rate must match federal minimum wage rate if the latter is greater.	Pennsylvania Statutes, 43 P.S. §333.104	"Except as may otherwise be provided under this act: (a) Every employer shall pay to each of his or her employees wages for all hours worked at a rate of not less than: (1) Two dollars sixty-five cents ($2.65) an hour upon the effective date of this amendment. (2) Two dollars ninety cents ($2.90) an hour during the year beginning January 1, 1979. (3) Three dollars ten cents ($3.10) an hour during the year beginning January 1, 1980. (4) Three dollars thirty-five cents ($3.35) an hour after December 31, 1980. (5) Three dollars seventy cents ($3.70) an hour beginning February 1, 1989, and thereafter. (6) Five dollars fifteen cents ($5.15) an hour beginning September 1, 1997. (7) Six dollars twenty-five cents ($6.25) an hour beginning January 1, 2007. (8) Seven dollars fifteen cents ($7.15) an hour beginning July 1, 2007.

State	State Minimum Wage Rate	Year Established / Year Effectivea	Mechanism of Setting State Rate	Mechanism for Future Adjustments	State Legislation or Policy Citation	Pertinent Language and Notes
						(a.1) If the minimum wage set forth in the Fair Labor Standards Act of 1938 (52 Stat. 1060, 29 U.S.C. §201 et seq.) is increased above the minimum wage required under this section, the minimum wage required under this section shall be increased by the same amounts and effective the same date as the increases under the Fair Labor Standards Act, and the provisions of subsection (a) are suspended to the extent they differ from those set forth under the Fair Labor Standards Act."
Rhode Island	$9.00	2014 / 2015	State specified rate of $9.00 on January 1, 2015.	None	Rhode Island General Laws 28-12-3	"(a) Every employer shall pay to each of his or her employees: commencing July 1, 1999, at least the minimum wage of five dollars and sixty five cents ($5.65) per hour. Commencing September 1, 2000, the minimum wage is six dollars and fifteen cents ($6.15) per hour. (b) Commencing January 1, 2004, the minimum wage is six dollars and seventy-five cents ($6.75) per hour. (c) Commencing March 1, 2006, the minimum wage is seven dollars and ten cents ($7.10) per hour.

Table A-1. (Continued)

State	State Minimum Wage Rate	Year Established / Year Effectivea	Mechanism of Setting State Rate	Mechanism for Future Adjustments	State Legislation or Policy Citation	Pertinent Language and Notes
						(d) Commencing January 1, 2007, the minimum wage is seven dollars and forty cents ($7.40) per hour. (e) Commencing January 1, 2013, the minimum wage is seven dollars and seventy-five cents ($7.75) per hour. (f) Commencing January 1, 2014, the minimum wage is eight dollars ($8.00) per hour. (g) Commencing January 1, 2015, the minimum wage is nine dollars ($9.00) per hour."
South Carolina	None	n/a	None	None	No state minimum wage law	n/a
South Dakota	$8.50	2014 / 2015	State specified rate of $8.50 on January 1, 2015, followed by adjustment on each successive January 1.	Inflation: CPI-U, U.S. City Average	South Dakota Code 60-11-3	"Every employer shall pay to each employee wages at a rate of not less than eight dollars and fifty cents an hour. Beginning January 1, 2016, and again on January 1 of each year thereafter, the minimum wage provided by § 60-11-3 shall be adjusted by the increase, if any, in the cost of living.

State	State Minimum Wage Rate	Year Established / Year Effectivea	Mechanism of Setting State Rate	Mechanism for Future Adjustments	State Legislation or Policy Citation	Pertinent Language and Notes
						The increase in the cost of living shall be measured by the percentage increase as of August of the immediately preceding year over the level as measured as of August of the previous year of the Consumer Price Index (all urban consumers, U.S. city average for all items) or its successor index as published by the U.S. Department of Labor or its successor agency, with the amount of the minimum wage increase, if any, rounded up to the nearest five cents. In no case shall the minimum wage be decreased. The Secretary of the South Dakota Department of Labor and Regulation or its designee shall publish the adjusted minimum wage rate for the forthcoming year on its internet home page by October 15 of each year, and it shall become effective on January 1 of the forthcoming year."
Tennessee	None	n/a	None	None	No state minimum wage law	n/a

Table A-1. (Continued)

State	State Minimum Wage Rate	Year Established / Year Effectivea	Mechanism of Setting State Rate	Mechanism for Future Adjustments	State Legislation or Policy Citation	Pertinent Language and Notes
Texas	$7.25	2001 / 2009	State specified rate equal to FLSA rate on September 1, 2001, thereafter equaling the FLSA rate.	Next FLSA minimum wage rate change.	Texas Labor Code Annotated 62.051	"Except as provided by Section 62.057, an employer shall pay to each employee the federal minimum wage under Section 6, Fair Labor Standards Act of 1938 (29 U.S.C. Section 206)."
Utah	$7.25	1990 / 2009	State specified rate of $3.80 on April 1, 1990.	Utah Labor Commission is authorized to review state minimum wage at any time and must review state minimum wage when FLSA rate is changed. The commission is prohibited from setting a rate above the FLSA rate.	Utah Code Annotated 34-40-103	"Minimum wage—Commission to review and modify minimum wage. (1)(a) The minimum wage for all private and public employees within the state shall be $3.35 per hour. (b) Effective April 1, 1990, the minimum wage shall be $3.80 per hour. (2)(a) After July 1, 1990, the commission may by rule establish the minimum wage or wages as provided in this chapter that may be paid to employees in public and private employment within the state. (b) The minimum wage, as established by the commission, may not exceed the federal minimum wage as provided in 29 U.S.C. Sec. 201 et seq.,

State	State Minimum Wage Rate	Year Established / Year Effectivea	Mechanism of Setting State Rate	Mechanism for Future Adjustments	State Legislation or Policy Citation	Pertinent Language and Notes
						the Fair Labor Standards Act of 1938, as amended, in effect at the time of implementation of this section."
Vermont	$9.15	2014 / 2015	State specified rate of $9.15 on January 1, 2015.	Scheduled increases: $9.60 (1-1-15) $10.00 (1-1-17) $10.50 (1-1-18) Beginning January 1, 2019, adjustment to be based on inflation (CPI-U, U.S. City Average) State rate must match federal minimum wage rate if the latter is greater.	Vermont Statutes Annotated, 21 Section 384	"(a) An employer shall not employ any employee at a rate of less than $9.15. Beginning January 1, 2016, an employer shall not employ any employee at a rate of less than $9.60. Beginning January 1, 2017, an employer shall not employ any employee at a rate of less than $10.00. Beginning January 1, 2018, an employer shall not employ any employee at a rate of less than $10.50, and beginning January 1, 2019 and on each subsequent January 1, the minimum wage rate shall be increased by five percent or the percentage increase of the Consumer Price Index, CPI-U, U.S. city average, not seasonally adjusted, or successor index, as calculated by the U.S. Department of Labor or successor agency for the 12 months preceding the previous September 1, whichever is smaller, but in no event shall the minimum wage be decreased.

Table A-1. (Continued)

State	State Minimum Wage Rate	Year Established / Year Effectivea	Mechanism of Setting State Rate	Mechanism for Future Adjustments	State Legislation or Policy Citation	Pertinent Language and Notes
						The minimum wage shall be rounded off to the nearest $0.01. An employer in the hotel, motel, tourist place, and restaurant industry shall not employ a service or tipped employee at a basic wage rate less than one-half the minimum wage. As used in this subsection, "a service or tipped employee" means an employee of a hotel, motel, tourist place, or restaurant who customarily and regularly receives more than $120.00 per month in tips for direct and personal customer service. If the minimum wage rate established by the U.S. government is greater than the rate established for Vermont for any year, the minimum wage rate for that year shall be the rate established by the U.S. government."

State	State Minimum Wage Rate	Year Established / Year Effectivea	Mechanism of Setting State Rate	Mechanism for Future Adjustments	State Legislation or Policy Citation	Pertinent Language and Notes
Virginia	$7.25	1991 / 2009	State specified rate equal to FLSA rate in 1997, thereafter equaling the FLSA rate.	Next FLSA minimum wage rate change.	Virginia Code Annotated 40.1-28.10	"Every employer shall pay to each of his employees wages at a rate not less than the federal minimum wage and a training wage as prescribed by the U.S. Fair Labor Standards Act (29 U.S.C. § 201 et seq.)." Note: This is language from the current statute as revised by 1997 legislation, but a 1991 law had already required that the state minimum wage match the federal rate.
Washington	$9.47	1998 / 2015	State specified rate of $6.50 on January 1, 2000, followed by adjustment on January 1, 2001, and each successive January 1.	Inflation: CPI-W	Revised Code of Washington 49.46.020	"On September 30, 2000, and on each following September 30th, the department of labor and industries shall calculate an adjusted minimum wage rate to maintain employee purchasing power by increasing the current year's minimum wage rate by the rate of inflation. The adjusted minimum wage rate shall be calculated to the nearest cent using the consumer price index for urban wage earners and clerical workers, CPI-W, or a successor index, for the twelve months prior to each September 1st as calculated by the United States department of labor.

Table A-1. (Continued)

State	State Minimum Wage Rate	Year Established / Year Effectivea	Mechanism of Setting State Rate	Mechanism for Future Adjustments	State Legislation or Policy Citation	Pertinent Language and Notes
						Each adjusted minimum wage rate calculated under this subsection (4)(b) takes effect on the following January 1st."
West Virginia	$8.00	2014 / 2015	State specified rate of $8.00 on January 1, 2015.	Scheduled increases: $8.75 (1-1-16) Note: State rate must match federal minimum wage rate if the latter is greater.	West Virginia Code 21-5C-2	"(a) Minimum wage: (1) After June 30, 2006, every employer shall pay to each of his or her employees wages at a rate not less than $ 5.85 per hour. (2) After June 30, 2007, every employer shall pay to each of his or her employees wages at a rate not less than $ 6.55 per hour. (3) After June 30, 2008, every employer shall pay to each of his or her employees wages at a rate not less than $ 7.25 per hour. (4) After January 1, 2015, every employer shall pay to each of his or her employees wages at a rate not less than $ 8.00 per hour. (5) After January 1, 2016, every employer shall pay to each of his or her employees wages at a rate not less than $ 8.75 per hour.

State	State Minimum Wage Rate	Year Established / Year Effectivea	Mechanism of Setting State Rate	Mechanism for Future Adjustments	State Legislation or Policy Citation	Pertinent Language and Notes
						(6) When the federal minimum hourly wage as prescribed by 29 U.S.C. Section 206(a)(1) is equal to or greater than the wage rate prescribed in the applicable provision of this subsection, every employer shall pay to each of his or her employees wages at a rate of not less than the federal minimum hourly wage as prescribed by 29 U.S.C. Section 206(a)(1). The minimum wage rates required under this subparagraph shall be thereafter adjusted in accordance with adjustments made in the federal minimum hourly rate. The adoption of the federal minimum wage provided by this subdivision includes only the federal minimum hourly rate prescribed in 29 U.S.C. Section 206(a)(1) and does not include other wage rates, or conditions, exclusions, or

Table A-1. (Continued)

State	State Minimum Wage Rate	Year Established / Year Effectivea	Mechanism of Setting State Rate	Mechanism for Future Adjustments	State Legislation or Policy Citation	Pertinent Language and Notes
						exceptions to the federal minimum hourly wage rate. In addition, adoption of the federal minimum hourly wage rate does not extend or modify the scope or coverage of the minimum wage rate required under this subdivision." Note: This is language from legislation signed into law in June 2014, but a 2006 law had already set the state minimum wage at $7.25, effective 6-30-08.
Wisconsin	$7.25	2009 / 2009	State specified rate of $7.25 on July 24, 2009.	None	Wisconsin Administrative Code 272.03	"This subsection is effective on July 24, 2009. Except as provided in ss. DWD 272.05 to 272.09, no employer may employ any employee in any occupation, trade, or industry at a lesser hourly rate than as follows: (a) All employees except opportunity and minor employees $7.25 per hour. (b) Minor employees $7.25 per hour. (c) Opportunity employees $5.90 per hour."

State	State Minimum Wage Rate	Year Established / Year Effective[a]	Mechanism of Setting State Rate	Mechanism for Future Adjustments	State Legislation or Policy Citation	Pertinent Language and Notes
Wyoming	$5.15	2001 / 2001	State specified rate of $5.15 on April 1, 2001.	None	Wyoming Statutes Annotated 27-4-202	"Every employer shall pay to each of his or her employees wages at a rate of not less than five dollars and fifteen cents ($5.15) per hour"

Source: Minimum wage rates are from U.S. Dept. of Labor, http://www.dol.gov/esa/minwage/america.htm; adjustment mechanisms are from state websites and National Conference of State Legislatures, http://www.ncsl.org/research/labor-and-employment policy citation and pertinent language are from state statutes.

[a] "Year Established" refers to the year that legislation or a ballot initiative establishing the current minimum wage rate in the state was passed. "Year Effective" refers to the year that the current minimum wage rate went into effect. While the majority of states have enacted minimum wage laws through state legislatures, the following 10 states' minimum wage provisions were established through ballot initiatives or referendum: Arizona, Colorado, Florida, Missouri, Montana, Nevada, New Jersey, Ohio, Oregon, and Washington.

[b] A ballot initiative to amend the Florida state constitution and establish a minimum wage was approved by voters in 2004; in 2005 legislation was passed (S.B. 18) that created a new section in the Florida Statutes: 448.110 (State Minimum Wage; Annual Wage Adjustment; Enforcement).

[c] Minnesota's $8.00 minimum wage rate applies to large employers, which are defined as enterprises "whose annual gross volume of sales made or business done is not less than $500,000 (exclusive of excise taxes at the retail level that are separately stated) and covered by the Minnesota Fair Labor Standards Act." Small employers (defined as enterprises "whose annual gross volume of sales made or business done is less than $500,000") may pay a minimum wage of $6.50. There are scheduled increases for small employers effective on the same dates as those for large employers.

[c] Nevada's $8.25 minimum wage rate applies to employees who do not receive health benefits. The minimum wage for employees who receive qualified health benefits from their employers is $7.25 per hour.

End Notes

[1] In addition, the FLSA provides for overtime pay and child labor protections. For a broader overview of the minimum wage, see CRS Report R43089, *The Federal Minimum Wage: In Brief*, by David H. Bradley.

[2] Although the rate has increased 22 separate times, this does not mean that there have been 22 separately enacted laws to increase the minimum wage. In some cases, one law contained multiple increases in the minimum wage rate that were phased in over time.

[3] 29 U.S.C. §206(a). State laws generally cover and exempt similar types of workers as those covered and exempted in the FLSA. While there are some cases in which state laws seem to cover different types or classes of workers than the FLSA, these coverage differentials appear to be relatively minor.

[4] The $500,000 threshold refers to the annual gross volume of sales. It is not a measure of net revenue or profits.

[5] U.S. Department of Labor, *Coverage Under the Fair Labor Standards Act*, available at http://www.dol.gov/whd/regs/ compliance/whdfs14.pdf. (Hereinafter cited as DOL, *Coverage Under the Fair Labor Standards Act*.) These examples are not exhaustive but are meant to illustrate the relatively broad range of activities comprising "interstate commerce."

[6] DOL provides a series of fact sheets on the various individual minimum wage exemptions in the FLSA. See http://www.dol.gov/whd/fact-sheets-index.htm for individual fact sheets.

[7] U.S. Department of Labor, Wage and Hour Division, Minimum Wage Laws in the States, http://www.dol.gov/whd/ minwage/america.htm and state web sites. See Appendix for details and sources.

[8] This figure is derived from the civilian labor force estimates from the Bureau of Labor Statistics (BLS) Local Area Unemployment Statistics (LAUS) program. Specifically, the August 2014 seasonally adjusted total civilian labor force in each state was totaled for the 29 states and D.C. with a minimum wage higher than the federal minimum wage. This total was then divided by the August 2014 seasonally adjusted civilian labor force for all states and D.C.

[9] States may also not provide any mechanism for future minimum wage changes. Of the 29 states and D.C. with minimum wages above the federal rate as of January 1, 2015, four—Illinois, Maine, New Mexico, and Rhode Island— do not provide a mechanism for future rate adjustment. Table A-1 provides details.

[10] For additional information about CPI, see http://www.bls.gov/cpi/cpiovrvw.htm.

[11] Following a series of scheduled increases, the Minnesota minimum wage rate will be indexed using the implicit price deflator for personal consumption expenditures, beginning in 2018.

[12] The mechanisms discussed here use the federal rate plus an add-on to set a state rate above the federal rate. Many states set the state rate to the federal rate, so that the state rate automatically changes when the federal rate changes.

[13] Because the prevailing federal minimum wage and state minimum wages go into effect at various points in a given year, the analysis in this section considers the years before and after federal changes have gone into effect. This is because the number of states with higher minimum wages may be different on January 1st of a given year than on December 31st of that same year. In order to avoid complications of within-year changes, the summaries in this section are based on rate increases that occurred any time during the year (e.g., the federal increase to $7.25 on July 24, 2009 is reflected as a rate of $7.25 for all of 2009). In addition, unless otherwise noted in this section, D.C. is counted as a state for simplicity of presentation.

[14] The federal minimum wage is the floor for "covered workers" (see previous discussion on enterprise and individual coverage) in these states. Generally, the great majority of workers are covered. For those who are not covered, the state minimum wage is likely to be the wage floor.

[15] Utah does not fit entirely into any of the four categories. Utah state law authorizes the Utah Labor Commissioner to set the state rate but prohibits the commissioner from setting a rate higher than the FLSA rate.

In: Minimum Wages
Editor: Vivian Haywood

ISBN: 978-1-63482-122-3

Chapter 2

THE FEDERAL MINIMUM WAGE: IN BRIEF*

David H. Bradley

SUMMARY

The Fair Labor Standards Act (FLSA), enacted in 1938, is the federal legislation that establishes the minimum hourly wage that must be paid to all covered workers. The minimum wage provisions of the FLSA have been amended numerous times since 1938, typically for the purpose of expanding coverage or raising the wage rate. Since its establishment, the minimum wage rate has been raised 22 separate times. The most recent change was enacted in 2007 (P.L. 110-28), which increased the minimum wage to its current level of $7.25 per hour.

In addition to setting the federal minimum wage rate, the FLSA provides for several exemptions and subminimum wage categories for certain classes of workers and types of work. Even with these exemptions, the FLSA minimum wage provisions still cover the vast majority of the workforce. Despite this broad coverage, however, the minimum wage directly affects a relatively small portion of the workforce. Currently, there are approximately 3.6 million workers, or 4.7% of all hourly paid workers, whose wages are at or below the federal minimum wage of $7.25 per hour. Approximately three-quarters of

* This is an edited, reformatted and augmented version of a Congressional Research Service publication, CRS Report for Congress R43089, dated January 17, 2014.

minimum wage workers are age 20 or older and nearly two-thirds work part time.

Proponents of increasing the federal minimum wage argue that it may increase earnings for lower income workers, lead to reduced turnover, and increase aggregate demand by providing greater purchasing power for workers receiving a pay increase. Opponents of increasing the federal minimum wage argue that it may result in reduced employment or reduced hours, lead to a general price increase, and reduce profits of firms paying a higher minimum wage.

The Federal Minimum Wage

The Fair Labor Standards Act (FLSA), enacted in 1938, is the federal legislation that establishes the general minimum wage that must be paid to all covered workers.[1] A full discussion of the coverage of the minimum wage is beyond the scope of this report, which provides only a broad overview of the topic. In general, the FLSA mandates broad general minimum wage coverage. It also specifies certain categories of workers who are not covered by FLSA wage standards, such as workers with disabilities or certain youth workers. The act was enacted because its provisions were meant to both protect workers and stimulate the economy. The FLSA also created the Wage and Hour Division (WHD), within the Department of Labor (DOL), to administer and enforce the act.

In 1938, the FLSA established a minimum wage of $0.25 per hour. The minimum wage provisions of the FLSA have been amended numerous times since then, typically for the purpose of expanding coverage or raising the wage rate. Since its establishment, the minimum wage rate has been raised 22 separate times.

The most recent change was enacted in 2007 (P.L. 110-28), which increased the minimum wage from $5.15 per hour to its current rate of $7.25 per hour in three steps. For employees working in states with a minimum wage different from that of the federal minimum wage, the employee is entitled to the higher wage of the two.

FLSA Minimum Wage Coverage

The FLSA extends minimum wage coverage to individuals under two types of coverage— "enterprise coverage" and "individual coverage."[2] An individual is covered if they meet the criteria for either category. Around 130 million workers, or 84% of the labor force, are covered by the FLSA.[3]

Enterprise Coverage

The first category of coverage is at the business or enterprise level. To be covered, an enterprise must have at least two employees and must have annual sales or "business done" of at least $500,000. Annual sales or business done includes all business activities that can be measured in dollars. Thus, for example, retailers are covered by the FLSA if their annual sales are at least $500,000.[4] In non-sales cases, such as enterprises engaged in leasing property, gross amounts paid by tenants for property rental will be considered "business done" for purposes of determining enterprise coverage.

In addition, regardless of the dollar volume of business, the FLSA applies to hospitals or other institutions primarily providing medical or nursing care for residents; schools (preschool through institutions of higher education); and federal, state, and local governments.

Individual Coverage

The second category of coverage is at the individual level. Although an enterprise may not be subject to minimum wage requirements if it has less than $500,000 in annual sales or business done, employees of the enterprise may be covered if they are individually engaged in interstate commerce or in the production of goods for interstate commerce. The definition of interstate commerce is fairly broad. To be engaged in "interstate commerce," employees must produce goods (or have indirect input to the production of those goods) that will be shipped out of the state of production, travel to other states for work, make phone calls or send emails to persons in other states, handle records that are involved in interstate transactions, or provide services to buildings (e.g., janitorial work) in which goods are produced for shipment outside of the state.[5]

Exemptions and Subminimum Wages

The FLSA covers most, but not all, private and public sector employees.[6] Certain employers and employees are exempt from all or parts of the FLSA minimum wage provisions, either through the individual or enterprise coverage or through specific exemptions included in the act. In addition, the FLSA provides for the payment of subminimum wages (i.e., less than the statutory rate of $7.25 per hour) for certain classes of workers.

Excluded from FLSA Minimum Wage Coverage

The FLSA statutorily exempts various workers from FLSA minimum wage coverage. Some of the exemptions are for a class of workers (e.g., executive, administrative, and professional employees), while others are more narrowly targeted to workers performing specific tasks (e.g., workers employed on a casual basis to provide babysitting services).

The list below is not exhaustive but is intended to provide examples of workers who are not covered by the minimum wage requirements of the FLSA:[7]

- bona fide executive, administrative, and professional employees;[8]
- individuals employed by certain establishments operating only part of the year (e.g., seasonal amusement parks, organized summer camps);
- individuals who are elected to state or local government offices and members of their staffs, policymaking appointees of elected officeholders of state or local governments, and employees of legislative bodies of state or local governments;
- employees who are immediate family members of an employer engaged in agriculture;
- individuals who volunteer their services to a private, nonprofit food bank and who receive groceries from the food bank;
- agricultural workers meeting certain hours and job duties requirements;
- individuals employed in the publication of small circulation newspapers;
- domestic service workers employed on a casual basis to provide babysitting;
- individuals employed to deliver newspapers; and
- certain employees in computer-related occupations.

Subminimum Wages

The FLSA also allows the payment of subminimum wages for certain classes of workers, including the following:

- **Youth.**[9] Employers may pay a minimum wage of $4.25 per hour to individuals under the age of 20 for the first 90 days of employment.
- **Learners.**[10] Employers may apply for special certificates from the Wage and Hour Division of DOL that allow them to pay students who are receiving instruction in an accredited school and are employed part-time as part of a vocational training program a wage at least 75% of the federal minimum wage ($5.44 at the current minimum wage).
- **Full-Time Students.**[11] Employers may apply for special certificates from the Wage and Hour Division of DOL that allow them to pay full-time students who are employed in retail or service establishments, an agricultural occupation, or an institution of higher education a wage at least 85% of the federal minimum wage ($6.16 at the current minimum wage).
- **Individuals with Disabilities.**[12] Employers may apply for special certificates from the Wage and Hour Division of DOL that allow them to pay wages lower than the otherwise applicable federal minimum to persons "whose earning or productive capacity is impaired by age, physical or mental deficiency, or injury." As elaborated in regulations, disabilities that may affect productive capacity include, but are not limited to, blindness, mental illness, mental retardation, cerebral palsy, alcoholism, and drug addiction. There is no statutory minimum wage required under this provision of the FLSA, but pay is to be broadly commensurate with pay to comparable non-disabled workers and related to the individual's productivity.[13]
- **Tipped Workers.**[14] Under Section 203(m) of the FLSA, a "tipped employee"—a worker who "customarily and regularly receives more than $30 a month in tips"—may have his or her cash wage from an employer reduced to $2.13 per hour, as long as the combination of tips and cash wage from the employer equals the federal minimum wage. An employer may count against his or her liability for the required payment of the full federal minimum wage the amount an employee earns in tips. The value of tips that an employer may count against their payment of the full minimum wage is known as the "tip credit." Under the current federal minimum wage and the current required minimum employer cash wage, the maximum tip credit is

$5.12 per hour (i.e., $7.25 minus $2.13). Thus, all workers covered under the tip credit provision of the FLSA are guaranteed the federal minimum wage.

Characteristics of Minimum Wage Workers

The most recent data available indicate that there are approximately 3.6 million workers, or 4.7% of all hourly paid workers, whose wages are at or below the federal minimum wage of $7.25 per hour. Of these 3.6 million workers, approximately 1.6 million earn the federal minimum wage of $7.25 per hour and the other 2 million earn below the federal minimum wage. As the Bureau of Labor Statistics (BLS) notes, the large number of individuals earning less than the statutory minimum wage does not necessarily indicate violations of the FLSA but may reflect exemptions or misreporting.[15]

Of the estimated 3.6 million workers earning at or below the minimum wage,

- about a quarter (24.1%) are teenagers (ages 16-19),
- nearly two-thirds (64.4%) are female,
- just over one-third (36%) are full-time workers (35 or more hours per week),
- more than 40% work in “food preparation and serving related occupations,”
- just over 15% work in “sales and related occupations,” and
- nearly three-quarters (72.2%) have at least a high school degree; overall, 8.0% have a bachelor’s degree or higher.

State Minimum Wages

States may also choose to set labor standards that are different from federal statutes. The FLSA establishes that if states enact minimum wage, overtime, or child labor laws more protective of employees than those provided in the FLSA, the state law applies. In the case of minimum wages, this means that if an individual is covered by the FLSA in a state with a higher state minimum wage, the individual is entitled to receive the higher state minimum wage. On the other hand, some states have set minimum wages lower than the FLSA minimum. In those cases, an FLSA-covered worker would receive the FLSA minimum wage and not the lower state minimum wage.

Currently, 21 states and the District of Columbia have minimum wage rates above the federal rate of $7.25 per hour. These rates range from $7.40 per hour in Michigan to $9.32 in Washington State. Four states have minimum wage rates below the federal rate and five have no minimum wage requirement. The remaining 20 states have minimum wage rates equal to the federal rate.[16] In the states with no minimum wage requirements or wages lower than the federal minimum wage, only individuals who are not covered by the FLSA are subject to those lower rates.

ARGUMENTS FOR AND AGAINST RAISING THE MINIMUM WAGE

The literature on the effects of the minimum wage is vast and represents one of the more well-studied issues in labor economics. As such, this topic has resulted in hundreds of academic and non-academic publications. It is beyond the scope of this section to summarize or synthesize this literature. Broadly speaking, there is not universal consensus on the causal relationship between changes in minimum wage and other economic outcomes. This section presents a brief summary of the primary arguments that proponents and opponents make regarding minimum wage increases.

Arguments for Increasing the Minimum Wage[17]

Increases Earnings

Proponents of an increase in the minimum wage often assert that raising wages can be a component in reducing poverty for individuals and families and a direct way to increase earnings for lower-income workers. Assuming the minimum wage earner does not suffer a loss of employment, hours, or other wage supplements as a result of the increase, then an increased minimum wage should close the gap between earnings and the poverty line. For example, a single parent with two children who works full-time, year-round at the current minimum wage has earnings of about 76% of the poverty line. An increase in the minimum wage to $9 per hour would raise that family's earnings to about 94% of the poverty line.[18]

Increases Aggregate Demand

Proponents of minimum wage increases also argue that additional income for individuals will result in increased aggregate demand in the economy. Adult minimum wage households have a higher marginal propensity to spend additional income than higher-income households. Therefore, to the extent that minimum wage increases raise the income of adult minimum wage households, a minimum wage increase could have a stimulative effect on the economy.

Reduces Inequality

Proponents of an increase in the minimum wage argue that it could help reduce earnings inequality by setting a higher floor at the lower end of the wage scale. At the level of an individual business, wage compression might occur if the minimum wage increases at the low end of the pay scale were offset by freezes or reductions in pay at higher levels of pay. That is, the spread between the lowest earners and the highest earners at a business might narrow if the business adjusted to higher pay for minimum wage earners by keeping flat or reducing pay for higher earners. Economy-wide, the size of the gap between low-wage earners and middle and high earners might decrease depending on how widely wage compression was used as a channel of adjustment to minimum wage increases.

Reduces Employee Turnover

A higher wage may lead workers to choose to stay in their jobs longer than they otherwise would have under a lower wage. Because high turnover is costly to businesses, proponents of minimum wage increases argue that an increase in the minimum wage may be offset by lower turnover costs.

Arguments against Increasing the Minimum Wage[19]

Reduces Employment

Much of the popular discussion about the effects of a minimum wage increase focuses only on one channel of adjustment—employment. In particular, opponents of a minimum wage or of minimum wage increases assert that increases in the minimum wage will result in increased unemployment, either broadly or for particular subpopulations of the labor market (e.g., youth, less skilled or experienced workers), or a reduction in hours worked. In a standard competitive model of the labor market, the introduction of or increase in the minimum wage (a price increase) results in employment losses (demand decrease).

Does Not Reduce Poverty

Because the minimum wage is not targeted to workers in low-income households, it is possible that the minimum wage does not reduce poverty to the extent a targeted policy might (e.g., tax credit). The minimum wage is a relatively blunt anti-poverty policy as it may raise wages for people not in poverty such as suburban teenagers who live in a middle- or high-income household.

Increases Prices

Another way minimum wage increases might be absorbed is through changes in prices. Specifically, employers facing a higher mandated minimum wage might choose, if possible, to pass on the extra costs of labor to the consumers through higher prices. If minimum wage increases result in an increase in the aggregate price level, then the inflationary effects would erode some of the purchasing power of both those receiving raises and everyone else in the economy.

Reduces Profits

A decrease in profits could be another means of adjustment to an increase in the minimum wage. The ability of any given business to lower profits to pay for mandated increases depends on the profit margins of that firm.

End Notes

[1] In addition, the FLSA provides for overtime pay and child labor protections. The scope of this report is only on the minimum wage provisions. For a broader overview of the FLSA, see CRS Report R42713, *The Fair Labor Standards Act (FLSA): An Overview*, by Gerald Mayer, Benjamin Collins, and David H. Bradley.

[2] 29 U.S.C. §206(a).

[3] U.S. Department of Labor, Wage and Hour Division, *Coverage Under the Fair Labor Standards Act (FLSA)*, Fact Sheet #14, Washington, DC, July 2009, http://www.dol.gov/whd/regs/compliance/whdfs14.pdf. Because some individuals are exempt from the minimum wage provisions of the FLSA, the number of workers covered by the minimum wage provisions is presumably lower.

[4] The $500,000 threshold refers to the annual gross volume of sales. It is not a measure of net revenue or profits.

[5] U.S. Department of Labor, *Coverage Under the Fair Labor Standards Act*, available at http://www.dol.gov/whd/regs/compliance/whdfs14.pdf. (Hereinafter cited as DOL, *Coverage Under the Fair Labor Standards Act.*) These examples are not exhaustive but are meant to illustrate the relatively broad range of activities comprising "interstate commerce."

[6] According to the WHD, "more than 130 million workers" are covered by the FLSA. Out of a total civilian labor force of about 155 million, this implies that about 84% of the workforce is covered.

[7] Most exemptions for individuals are in 29 U.S.C. §203(e), 29 U.S.C. §213(a), and 29 U.S.C. §213(d). The list here should not be considered exhaustive as there are various job duties, earnings, and employer characteristic requirements that further define the general exemptions listed here.

[8] The term "bona fide" indicates that job titles alone do not determine exempt status. Rather, employees falling under this exemption must meet criteria related to job duties and pay. See U.S. Department of Labor, Wage and Hour Division, *Exemption for Executive, Administrative, Professional, Computer & Outside Sales Employees Under the Fair Labor Standards Act (FLSA)*, Fact Sheet #17A, Washington, DC, July 2008, http://www.dol.gov/whd/regs/compliance/fairpay/fs17a_overview.pdf.

[9] 29 U.S.C. §206(g).

[10] 29 U.S.C. §214(a).

[11] 29 U.S.C. §214(b).

[12] 29 U.S.C. §214(c).

[13] For details on the process for determining wages under Section 14(c), see U.S. Department of Labor, Wage and Hour Division, *Prevailing Wages and Commensurate Wages under Section 14(c) of the Fair Labor Standards Act (FLSA)*, Fact Sheet #39B, Washington, DC, May 2009, http://www.dol.gov/whd/regs/compliance/whdfs39b.pdf.

[14] 29 U.S.C. §203(m).

[15] Bureau of Labor Statistics (BLS), U.S. Department of Labor, *Characteristics of Minimum Wage Workers: 2012*, Washington, DC, February 26, 2013, http://www.bls.gov/cps/minwage2012.pdf. BLS produces an annual report on minimum wage workers using data from the Current Population Survey (CPS), which is a monthly household survey used to collect economic and demographic information on the population. The CPS does not ask respondents directly if they earn the minimum wage. Rather the estimate of workers at or below the federal minimum wage is derived from reported earnings on a person's sole (or principal) job. As BLS notes, because the estimates are based on workers paid at hourly rates, with salaried and non-hourly workers excluded, "the actual number of workers with earnings at or below the prevailing minimum wage is undoubtedly understated."

[16] U.S. Department of Labor, Wage and Hour Division, *Minimum Wage Laws in the States*, http://www.dol.gov/whd/ minwage/america.htm.

[17] For examples of arguments in favor of increasing the federal minimum wage, see David Cooper and Doug Hall, *Raising the Federal Minimum Wage to $10.10 Would Give Working Families, and the Overall Economy, A Much-Needed Boost*, Economic Policy Institute, Briefing Paper #357, Washington, DC, March 13, 2013, http://www.epi.org/files/2013/bp357--federal-minimum-wage-increase.pdf and Christian E. Weller and Nick Bunker, *A Higher Minimum Wage Will Not Hurt U.S. Businesses*, Center for American Progress, Washington, DC, February 15, 2013, http://www.americanprogress.org/issues/economy/news/2013/02/15/53603/a-higher-minimum-wage-will-not-hurt-u-s-businesses/.

[18] These figures, produced by CRS, are based on estimated 2014 poverty thresholds. For a family of three the poverty threshold is $19,820. At the current minimum wage of $7.25 per hour, a full-time, year-round worker would earn $15,080, or 76% of this threshold. At a minimum wage of $9.00 per hour, a full-time, year-round worker would earn $18,720, or 94% of this threshold.

[19] For examples of arguments against increasing the federal minimum wage, see Mark Wilson, *The Negative Effects of Minimum Wage Laws*, Cato Institute, Washington, DC, September 2012, http://www.downsizinggovernment.org/sites/downsizinggovernment.org/files/pdf/negative-effects-minimum-wage-laws.pdf and James Sherk, *Who Earns the Minimum Wage? Suburban Teenagers, Not Single Parents*, The Heritage Foundation, Issue Brief No. 3866, Washington, DC, March 1, 2013, http://thf_media.s3.amazonaws.com/2013/pdf/ib3866.pdf.

In: Minimum Wages
Editor: Vivian Haywood

ISBN: 978-1-63482-122-3

Chapter 3

THE FAIR LABOR STANDARDS ACT (FLSA): AN OVERVIEW*

Gerald Mayer, Benjamin Collins and David H. Bradley

SUMMARY

The Fair Labor Standards Act (FLSA) provides workers with minimum wage, overtime pay, and child labor protections. The FLSA covers most, but not all, private and public sector employees. In addition, certain employers and employees are exempt from coverage.

Provisions of the FLSA that are of current interest to Congress include the basic minimum wage, subminimum wage rates, exemptions from overtime and the minimum wage for certain persons who provide companionship services, the exemption for certain employees in computer-related occupations, compensatory time ("comp time") in lieu of overtime pay, and break time for nursing mothers.

Basic Minimum Wage

- The FLSA requires employers to pay covered, nonexempt employees at least the minimum wage. In 2007, the basic minimum wage was raised, in steps, from $5.15 to $7.25 an hour. The basic minimum

* This is an edited, reformatted and augmented version of a Congressional Research Service publication, CRS Report for Congress R42713, dated January 2, 2014.

wage was raised to $7.25 an hour effective July 24, 2009. As of January 1, 2014, 21 states and the District of Columbia have minimum wage rates that are higher than the federal minimum wage.

- Basic minimum wage rates in American Samoa and the Commonwealth of the Northern Mariana Islands (CNMI) are lower than in the continental United States. In 2007, Congress passed the Fair Minimum Wage Act of 2007 (P.L. 110-28), which mandated annual increases of $0.50 an hour in the minimum wages of American Samoa and CNMI. In 2010, Congress temporarily suspended these increases. The minimum wage in CNMI increased by $0.50 an hour to $5.55 on September 30, 2012, and is scheduled to rise to $6.05 an hour on September 30, 2014. In July 2012, Congress delayed the wage increases in American Samoa. The next minimum wage increases in American Samoa are scheduled for September 30, 2015.

Subminimum Wage Rates

- Tipped employees may be paid less than the basic minimum wage, but their cash wage plus tips must equal at least the basic minimum wage of $7.25. Employers may pay tipped workers $2.13 an hour in cash wages, provided the employees receive at least $5.12 an hour in tips. The latter amount is called a "tip credit."
- Employers may pay special minimum wages (SMWs) to workers with disabilities. The purpose of the SMWs is to provide persons with disabilities the opportunity to work.

Overtime

- The FLSA requires employers to pay at least time-and-a-half to covered, nonexempt employees who work more than 40 hours in a week at a given job.
- The FLSA allows covered, nonexempt state and local government employees to receive compensatory time off (comp time) for hours worked over 40 in a workweek. Comp time is time off with pay in lieu of overtime pay.

Exemptions

- The FLSA exempts certain employers and employees from the minimum wage, overtime pay, or child labor standards of the act.
- Certain employees in computer-related occupations are exempt from both the minimum wage and overtime standards of the FLSA if they meet an hourly wage or weekly salary test and a job duties test.
- Domestic service workers who provide companionship services in private homes are exempt from both the minimum wage and overtime requirements of the FLSA if they are employed directly by an individual or family.

Under new regulations published in the *Federal Register* on October 1, 2013, minimum wage and overtime coverage now applies to companions who work in private households if they are employed by a third party. Overtime pay now applies to live-in domestic service workers who are employed by a third party.

In 1937, the United States was recovering from the Great Depression. As part of the recovery effort, President Franklin D. Roosevelt endorsed a series of economic programs, known as the New Deal, to help stimulate and rebuild the U.S. economy. The National Industrial Recovery Act (NIRA) was the major statute enacted to help achieve these goals. Although the NIRA was eventually found unconstitutional, many of its provisions appeared in later New Deal statutes, including in the Fair Labor Standards Act of 1938 (FLSA).[1]

The Fair Labor Standards Act[2]

The FLSA provides for a federal minimum wage, overtime pay, and child labor protections. Congress endorsed the act because its provisions were meant to both protect workers and stimulate the economy. The FLSA also created the Wage and Hour Division (WHD) within the Department of Labor (DOL) to administer and enforce the act.[3]

At the time of the act's passage, Congress found that a few employers who paid substandard wages caused a decrease in wages within their respective industries, because other employers sought to compete in the marketplace with lower priced goods.[4] Congress also found that these decreased wages caused one-third of the U.S. population to be "ill-nourished, ill-clad, and ill-housed."[5]

To counter these conditions, in 1938 Congress established a minimum wage of $0.25 an hour, gradually increasing to $0.40 an hour in 1945.[6] Congress has since legislated several increases in the minimum wage. It now stands at $7.25 an hour.

The FLSA also mandates a pay rate of one-and-one-half times an employee's hourly wage for every hour the employee works beyond a standard work week. When enacted, the FLSA required employers to pay overtime for hours worked in excess of 44 hours in a week.[7] The 44-hour threshold was lowered to 40 hours in 1940. The purpose of the overtime provision is to reduce unemployment by encouraging employers to hire more workers, rather than requiring current employees to work more than 40 hours per week and pay the premium overtime rate.

Finally, under the FLSA Congress set certain conditions under which children could work. Not only was oppressive child labor considered immoral, as children often worked at the cost of their own health and education, but Congress also believed that the lower wages generally earned by children drove down the wages of adult workers.[8]

The FLSA extends minimum wage, overtime pay, and child labor protections to individuals "employed by an employer."[9] Congress has also "exempted" certain employers and employees from all or parts of the FLSA. For example, exemptions were provided to executive, administrative, or professional (EAP) employees; individuals employed at retail stores that did not have interstate operations; and agricultural employees. Additionally, the child labor provisions did not apply to children employed in the motion picture or theater industries.[10]

WHO IS COVERED BY THE FLSA?

The FLSA covers employees and enterprises engaged in interstate commerce. An enterprise is covered if it has annual sales or business done of at least $500,000.[11] Regardless of the dollar volume of business, the act applies to hospitals; institutions primarily engaged in the care of the sick, aged, mentally ill, or disabled who reside on the premises; schools for children who are mentally or physically disabled or gifted; federal, state, and local governments; and preschools, elementary and secondary schools, and institutions of higher education.[12]

Although enterprises that have *less than* $500,000 in annual sales or business done are not covered by the FLSA, employees of these enterprises may be covered if they are individually engaged in interstate commerce. These employees may travel to other states for work, make phone calls or send emails to persons in other states, or handle records that are involved in interstate transactions.[13]

The $500,000 enterprise threshold has not been raised since it was enacted in 1989. Employers are required to administer dual enterprise and individual tests to determine if individual employees are covered by the act. That is, although an enterprise may not be covered if it has less than $500,000 in annual sales or business done, employees of the enterprise may be covered if they are individually engaged in interstate commerce.

The FLSA covers most, but not all, private and public sector employees. Persons who are not covered by the FLSA include individuals who are elected to state or local government offices and members of their staffs, policymaking appointees of elected officeholders of state or local governments, employees of legislative bodies of state or local governments, immediate family members of an employer engaged in agriculture, persons who volunteer their services to a state or local government (if the person is not employed by the government agency to perform the same services), and persons who volunteer their services to a private, nonprofit food bank and who receive groceries from the food bank.[14]

The FLSA exempts certain employers and employees from the minimum wage, overtime, or child labor standards of the act. For example, bona fide executive, administrative, and professional employees are exempt from both the minimum wage and overtime requirements of the act if they meet both a salary test and a job duties test. Certain employees in computer-related occupations are also exempt from both the minimum wage and overtime if they meet an hourly wage or weekly salary test and a job duties test. Domestic service workers who provide companionship services in private homes are exempt from both the minimum wage and overtime if they are employed directly by an individual or family.

RELATION OF THE FLSA TO STATE LAWS

Under Section 18 of the FLSA, if states enact minimum wage, overtime, or child labor laws that are more protective of employees than what is provided by the FLSA, the state law applies. The FLSA defines a state as "any State of the United States or the District of Columbia or any Territory or possession of the United States."[15] Because states may enact laws that are more protective of employees than what is provided by the FLSA, there are multiple minimum wage, overtime, and child labor standards nationwide.

MINIMUM WAGE RATES

Under Section 6 of the FLSA, employers must pay covered, nonexempt employees at least $7.25 an hour.[16] However, the FLSA includes several subminimum wage rates. Employers may pay lower minimum wage rates to tipped employees; workers with disabilities; new hires under the age of 20; full-time students who work in retail or service establishments, agriculture, or institutions of higher education; and high school students who are at least 16 years of age and enrolled in a vocational education program.

The Basic Minimum Wage

The basic minimum wage is raised periodically by Congress. The current basic minimum wage of $7.25 went into effect on July 24, 2009.[17] As of January 1, 2014, 21 states and the District of Columbia have minimum wage rates that are higher than the federal minimum wage.[18]

Most employees are paid more than the basic minimum wage. According to the Bureau of Labor Statistics (BLS), in 2012 95.3% of employees who were paid by the hour were paid an hourly wage that was greater than the federal minimum wage of $7.25.[19]

Tipped Workers

Tipped employees may be paid less than the basic minimum wage, but their cash wage plus tips must equal at least the basic minimum wage.

Under Section 3(m) of the FLSA, a “tipped employee” is a worker who “customarily and regularly” receives more than $30 a month in tips. Employers must allow tipped employees to keep all tips. However, the FLSA allows tips to be pooled and shared among tipped employees.

Under the FLSA, an employer may pay a tipped worker a minimum cash wage of $2.13 if the employee receives at least $5.12 an hour in tips (for a total hourly wage of $7.25).[20] Employers may claim up to $5.12 in tips as a tip credit. However, if a tipped employee receives less than $5.12 an hour in tips, the employer must make up the difference with a higher cash wage. For example, if a tipped employee receives $3.00 an hour in tips, the employer must pay the employee a cash wage of at least $4.25 an hour.

In states with a minimum wage that is higher than the federal minimum wage, the tip credit may be more than $5.12. On the other hand, as of January 1, 2012, seven states and Guam do not allow employers to claim a tip credit (i.e., employers must pay all tipped employees a cash wage that is at least the higher of the federal or state minimum wage). In 24 states and the District of Columbia, the minimum cash wage for tipped employees is greater than the federal minimum cash wage of $2.13. In 13 states and the Virgin Islands, the minimum cash wage for tipped employees is $2.13. In the remaining six states, five do not have state minimum wage laws and one exempts tipped employees from state law.[21]

Workers with Disabilities

Under Section 14(c) of the FLSA, employers may pay special minimum wages (SMWs) to workers with disabilities. The purpose of the SMWs is to provide persons with disabilities the opportunity to work. A disability may be physical or mental. It may be related to age or an injury. Disabilities include blindness, mental illness or retardation, alcoholism, and drug addiction.[22]

Employers must receive certificates from the Wage and Hour Division (WHD) of DOL that authorize the employers to pay SMWs.[23] WHD issues certificates to four types of employers: work centers, hospital or residential care facilities, businesses, and School Work Exploration Programs (SWEP). Work centers (also called "community rehabilitation programs" and "sheltered workshops") provide employment, training, and rehabilitation services. Hospital or residential care facilities employ "patient workers," who are employed persons who also receive treatment or care. A business establishment that employs workers with disabilities at SMWs must receive a certificate from WHD. Under SWEP, schools place students with disabilities at work sites in the community.

In order to pay a disabled worker less than the basic minimum wage, the employee's disabilities must impair his or her productive capacity in the job being performed. The wages paid must be "commensurate" to the worker's productivity. The worker's wage must be based on the worker's productivity relative to the wages and productivity of experienced workers who are not disabled and who perform the same type and quality of work in the same geographic area. For disabled workers paid an hourly wage, employers must review the workers' productivity, and adjust their wages accordingly, at least every six months. The wages of all disabled workers must also be adjusted at least once a year to take into account changes in wages paid to experienced, nondisabled workers.[24]

An employee paid a SMW, or the employee's parent or guardian, may ask WHD to review the wage paid to the employee.

New Hires under the Age of 20

Under what is known as the "youth opportunity wage," employers may pay a minimum wage of $4.25 an hour to employees under the age of 20 for their first 90 consecutive calendar days of employment.[25] Hiring youth at a subminimum wage cannot displace other workers. After 90 consecutive days of employment or when the worker reaches age 20, whichever comes first, the employee must be paid at least the basic minimum wage.

The purpose of the youth subminimum wage is to provide employment opportunities to young persons, especially disadvantaged youth. Some policy makers question whether it is appropriate to pay subminimum wage rates to persons under 20, especially if they have held other jobs.

Full-Time Students

Under Section 14(b) of the FLSA, employers may pay certain full-time students 85% of the basic minimum wage. The subminimum wage for full-time students applies to students employed by retail or service stores, in agriculture, or by institutions of higher education. Again, the purpose of the subminimum wage for full-time students is to provide these students with opportunities for employment. The FLSA does not impose an age limit on the subminimum wage for full-time students.

Student Learners

Under Section 14(a) of the FLSA, employers may pay "student learners" 75% of the basic minimum wage. Student learners are high school students who are (1) at least 16 years old (or 18 if employed in an occupation that the

Secretary of Labor has declared to be particularly hazardous for the employment of youth), (2) are receiving instruction in an accredited school, college, or university, and (3) are employed part-time by an employer as part of a vocational training program. The employer may pay student learners a subminimum wage for as long as the students are enrolled in the vocational education program. Employers must obtain certificates from DOL authorizing them to pay less than the basic minimum wage.[26]

Minimum Wage Rates in the Territories and Possessions of the United States

When the FLSA was enacted in 1938, the minimum wage in Guam, Puerto Rico, and the Virgin Islands was set at the same rate as in the continental United States ($0.25 an hour).[27] The minimum wage that applies in the continental United States has applied to Guam since 1938. However, in 1940 Congress enacted legislation that allowed Special Industry Committees (SICs) to set minimum wage rates by industry in Puerto Rico and the Virgin Islands. In 1989, Congress enacted legislation that eliminated the SIC structure in both territories. The minimum wage in the Virgin Islands has been the same as in the continental United States since 1989. In Puerto Rico, minimum wages by industry were raised, in steps, until they were the same as in the continental United States by April 1, 1996.

American Samoa and the Commonwealth of the Northern Mariana Islands (CNMI) were not covered by the FLSA of 1938. In 1956, Congress enacted legislation that required the Secretary of Labor to establish minimum wages in American Samoa based on recommendations from SICs. In 2007, Congress passed the Fair Minimum Wage Act of 2007 (P.L. 110-28).[28] For American Samoa, the act mandated annual increases of $0.50 an hour until the minimum wage in each industry reached the federal minimum wage. However, in 2010 Congress passed legislation (P.L. 111-244) that postponed the planned increases for 2010 and 2011.[29] In July 2012, Congress passed, and the President signed, the Insular Areas Act of 2011 (P.L. 112-149). The act delayed the increases in the minimum wages in American Samoa for 2012, 2013, and 2014. The next minimum wage increases in American Samoa are scheduled for September 30, 2015. Thereafter, increases will be made every three years until they reach the federal minimum wage.[30]

In the mid 1970s, the United States and CNMI entered into a Covenant of Association. CNMI retained control over the minimum wage in the islands.

However, as was the case with American Samoa, P.L. 110-28 mandated that the minimum wage in CNMI be raised by $0.50 a year until it reached the same level as in the continental United States. However, P.L. 111-244 eliminated the scheduled increase for 2011. On September 30, 2012, the minimum wage in CNMI increased by $0.50 an hour to $5.55.[31] In September 2013, Congress canceled the increases scheduled for 2013 and 2015. The minimum wage in CNMI is currently scheduled to rise by $0.50 an hour, to $6.05, on September 30, 2014.[32]

OVERTIME

Under Section 7, employers must pay covered workers at least one-and-a-half times their regular hourly wage for hours worked over 40 hours a week at a given job. Employers may choose to pay more than time-and-a-half for overtime or to pay overtime to employees who are exempt from overtime under the FLSA.

Under the FLSA, overtime pay applies to hours worked in excess of 40 in a workweek. Thus, the law allows some flexibility in work hours. For example, an employer could schedule four 10-hour workdays in a workweek without asking employees to work overtime. Similarly, an employee who works a five-day workweek could work four hours one day and nine hours the other four days and not work overtime.[33]

Comp Time in Lieu of Overtime Pay

The FLSA, under Section 7(o), allows covered, nonexempt state and local government employees to receive compensatory time off ("comp time") for hours worked over 40 in a workweek.[34] Comp time is time off with pay in lieu of overtime pay. An employer and employees must agree that the employer will provide comp time. The agreement may be through a collective bargaining agreement or, if there is no such agreement, between the employer and individual employees. Comp time is calculated at a rate that is at least one-and-a-half times the number of overtime hours worked. In general, state and local government employees may accrue up to 240 hours of comp time. Law enforcement, fire protection, emergency response personnel, and employees engaged in seasonal activities may accrue up to 480 hours of comp time. Instead of providing comp time, an employer may pay an employee for any unused comp time. An employee must be allowed to use comp time on the date requested, unless doing so would "unduly disrupt" the operations of the agency.[35] Section 7(o) does not apply to state and local government employees who are exempt from overtime.[36]

Break Time for Nursing Mothers

The Patient Protection and Affordable Care Act (PPACA, P.L. 111-148) added new Section 7(r) to the FLSA.[37] Section 7 of the FLSA requires employers to pay at least time-and-a-half to employees who work overtime. Section 13 of the FLSA provides several exemptions to the overtime requirements of Section 7. Thus, new Section 7(r) does not apply to employers or employees who are exempt from overtime.

Section 7(r) requires covered employers to provide break time for nursing mothers. Break time must be provided for one year after the child's birth. Employers must provide space, other than a bathroom, that is shielded from view and free from intrusion from coworkers and the public. Only employees who are not exempt from the FLSA's overtime pay requirements are entitled to break times to express milk. Employers with fewer than 50 employees are not subject to the requirement if compliance would impose an undue hardship on the employer. Employers are not required to compensate nursing mothers for breaks taken for the purpose of expressing milk.

Exemptions from the Minimum Wage or Overtime Standards of the FLSA

Most wage and salary workers are covered by the FLSA. However, under Section 13 of the act certain employers and employees are exempt from coverage. They may be exempt from either the minimum wage or overtime standards of the act, or both. This section considers some, but not all, of the current exemptions in Section 13. The focus is on those exemptions that have been the subject of recent legislation, hearings, or oversight.

Executive, Administrative, and Professional Employees

When the Fair Labor Standards Act (P.L. 75-718) was enacted in 1938, Section 13(a)(1) provided an exemption, from both the minimum wage and overtime requirements of the act, for bona fide executive, administrative, and professional employees (the EAP exemption).[38] The act did not define the terms executive, administrative, or professional employee. Instead, the law stated that the terms would be defined in regulations issued by the Secretary of Labor.[39]

Under current regulations, to qualify for the EAP exemption, employees must meet certain duties tests and be paid a salary of at least $455 per week.[40] Job titles do not determine whether an employee is exempt.

To qualify for the exemption for executive employees, all of the following job duties tests must be met:

- The employee's primary duty "is management of the enterprise in which the employee is employed or of a customarily recognized department or subdivision thereof";
- The employee "customarily and regularly directs the work of two or more other employees"; and
- The employee "has the authority to hire or fire other employees or whose suggestions and recommendations as to the hiring, firing, advancement, promotion or any other change of status of other employees are given particular weight."[41]

To qualify for the exemption for administrative employees, both of the following job duties tests must be met:

- The employee's primary duty "is the performance of office or nonmanual work directly related to the management or general business operations of the employer or the employer's customers"; and
- The employee's primary duty "includes the exercise of discretion and independent judgment with respect to matters of significance."[42]

To qualify for the exemption for professional employees, the following job duties test must be met:

- The employee's primary duty is the performance of work: "Requiring knowledge of an advanced type in a field of science or learning customarily acquired by a prolonged course of specialized intellectual instruction"; or "Requiring invention, imagination, originality or talent in a recognized field of artistic or creative endeavor."[43]

Periodically, DOL has modified the regulations that implement the EAP exemption. The regulations were last changed in 2004. The current minimum weekly salary of $455 is an issue in implementing the exemption. Between changes in the threshold, weekly salaries may rise because of inflation or increases in labor productivity. Thus, unless the threshold is raised (either legislatively or administratively), over time more employees become exempt from overtime pay. On the other hand, a higher threshold may make it more difficult for employers to administer overtime (i.e., because employers would have to keep track of hours worked for more employees).

The job duties tests are a second issue in implementing the EAP exemption. For an employee to be exempt, the employee's job duties must meet the requirements for exemption. The tests are complex and can result in workers being misclassified (e.g., they may be classified as exempt when they should be nonexempt). For employers, a higher salary threshold may make it easier to administer the job duties tests for exemption—because fewer employees would meet the minimum salary test.

Outside Salespersons

Outside salespersons are also exempt under Section 13(a)(1) of the FLSA. Unlike executive, administrative, and professional employees, however, the $455 salary test does not apply to outside salespersons.

To qualify for the exemption for outside sales employees, an employee must meet both of the following job duties tests:

- The employee's primary duty must be making sales (as defined in the FLSA), or obtaining orders or contracts for services or for the use of facilities for which a consideration will be paid by the client or customer;[44] and
- The employee must be customarily and regularly engaged away from the employer's place or places of business.[45]

An outside salesperson is someone who makes sales at the customer's home or place of business. The person may work hours that are convenient for the customer. Also, the hours worked by outside salespersons may be difficult for employers to monitor.

One issue with the exemption for outside salespersons is whether a sale involves the actual transfer of ownership of a company's goods or services. In a June 2012 decision by the U.S. Supreme Court, the court ruled that pharmaceutical sales representatives (also called "detailers") who encourage doctors to prescribe the use of a company's prescription drugs are outside salespersons, even though the drugs can only be sold with a doctor's prescription.[46]

Currently, regulations state that "Outside sales does not include sales made by mail, telephone or the Internet unless such contact is used merely as an adjunct to personal calls."[47] Some policy makers maintain that inside salespersons, whose primary duty is to make sales, should also be exempt.

Employees in Computer-Related Occupations

In 1990, Congress directed the Secretary of Labor to issue regulations that would exempt from overtime and the minimum wage certain employees in computer-related occupations.[48] Before 1990, computer employees could be exempt from FLSA coverage if they met the requirements of the EAP exemption. Regulations in effect in 1990 stated that the exemption for learned professionals applied to employees who have acquired "knowledge of an advanced type in a field of science or learning customarily acquired by a prolonged course of specialized intellectual instruction and study." The regulations said that knowledge of an "advanced type" was knowledge that generally could not be attained with only a high school degree. Rather, learned professionals typically held an "academic degree." The 1990 regulations went on to say that

> The question arises whether computer programmers and systems analysts in the data processing field are included in the learned professions. At the present time there is too great a variation in standards and academic requirements to conclude that employees employed in such occupations are a part of a true profession recognized as such by the academic community with universally accepted standards for employment in the field.[49]

In 1990, Congress enacted legislation that directed the Secretary of Labor to issue regulations that would allow "computer systems analysts, computer programmers, software engineers, and other similarly skilled professional workers" to qualify as exempt executive, administrative, or professional employees under Section 13(a)(1) of the FLSA. The 1990 legislation also directed the Secretary of Labor to apply the EAP exemption to employees in computer-related occupations if they were paid on an hourly wage that was at least six-and-a-half times the basic federal minimum wage.

In 1992, the U.S. Department of Labor (DOL) published final regulations that implemented the 1990 legislation. The regulations treated computer employees as professional employees under the EAP exemption. The regulations stated that the exemption applied to "highly skilled" computer employees. To be exempt as a professional employee, the 1992 regulations said that a computer employee's primary duty must consist of one or more of the following job duties:

(1) The application of systems analysis techniques and procedures, including consulting with users, to determine hardware, software, or system functional specifications;
(2) The design, development, documentation, analysis, creation, testing, or modification of computer systems or programs, including prototypes, based on and related to user or system design specifications;
(3) The design, documentation, testing, creation or modification of computer programs related to machine operating systems; or
(4) a combination of the aforementioned duties, the performance of which requires the same level of skills.

Finally, the 1992 regulations stated that "While such employees commonly have a bachelor's or higher degree, no particular academic degree is required for this exemption."[50]

When the final regulations implementing the 1990 legislation went into effect, the basic federal minimum wage was $4.25 an hour. Thus, computer employees who were paid by the hour were exempt if they met the new job duties test and were paid at least $27.63 an hour (i.e., 6½ times $4.25).

In 1996, Congress added Section 13(a)(17) to the FLSA. Section 13(a)(17) applies specifically to employees in computer-related occupations. Under Section 13(a)(17), the minimum hourly wage for computer professionals was fixed at $27.63 an hour. The exemption includes in statute much of the language from the 1992 regulations that defined the primary duties of exempt computer professionals.

In 2004, DOL issued new regulations that revised the salary and duties tests for the EAP exemption. The regulations also simplified the duties tests for computer professionals to reflect the 1996 amendments to the FLSA. Under the 2004 regulations, computer professionals are exempt from the minimum wage and overtime standards of the FLSA if they meet the job duties test provided in regulations and, if they are paid an hourly wage, are paid at least $27.63 an hour or, if they are paid a salary, are paid at least $455 a week.[51] The same duties tests apply to both salaried and hourly computer employees.[52]

Skilled computer workers are not necessarily exempt from the minimum wage or overtime requirements of the FLSA. Employees engaged in the manufacture or repair of computer hardware are not exempt. Employees whose work is highly dependent on the use of computers and computer software programs (e.g., engineers, drafters, and others skilled in computer-aided design software), but who are not primarily engaged in computer systems analysis and programming, are not exempt computer professionals.[53]

Domestic Service Employees

When the FLSA was enacted in 1938, it covered domestic service employees employed by a business or agency subject to the FLSA. It did not cover domestic service workers employed in private households. The Fair Labor Standards Amendments of 1974 (P.L. 93-259) extended minimum wage and overtime coverage to include domestic service workers who are employed in private homes.[54] Domestic service workers include housekeepers, cooks, gardeners, full-time babysitters, and others.[55]

In addition to extending minimum wage and overtime coverage to domestic service employees employed in private households, the 1974 amendments added two exemptions that affect two types of domestic service workers: domestic service workers who provide companionship services and live-in domestic service workers. Under Section 13(a)(15) of the FLSA, domestic service workers who provide companionship services in private homes are exempt from both the minimum wage and overtime standards of the act. Section 13(b)(21) of the act exempts from overtime, but not the minimum wage, domestic service workers who provide live-in domestic services.

On October 1, 2013, DOL published in the *Federal Register* new regulations that changed the definition of companionship services and limited the minimum wage and overtime exemptions for domestic service workers employed in private home to those workers who are employed directly by an individual or family. The new regulations go into effect on January 1, 2015.[56]

Under previous regulations:

- Companionship services were defined as "those services which provide fellowship, care, and protection for a person who, because of advanced age or physical or mental infirmity, cannot care for his or her own needs."
- Companionship services could include household work related to the care of the aged or infirmed individual, such as preparing meals, bed making, or washing clothes. Companionship services could also include general household work (such as housecleaning), if the work was "incidental" to providing companionship services. Prior regulations defined incidental as 20% or less of the total hours worked.
- Companionship services did not include services performed by trained personnel, such as registered or practical nurses.[57]

The new regulations narrow the definition of companionship services. Under the new rule:

- The definition of companionship services is limited to fellowship and protection (eliminating the reference to "care"). Fellowship includes social, physical, and mental activities, such as conversation, reading, games, crafts, or accompanying the person on walks, to appointments, or to social events. Protection means to be present with the person in their home or accompanying the person outside the home to monitor their safety and well-being.
- Companions can spend up to 20% of total hours worked per person per week on care that is "attendant to and in conjunction with the provision of fellowship and protection." Providing care means assisting the person with activities of daily living (such as dressing, grooming, feeding, bathing, and toileting) and instrumental activities of daily living (which are tasks that allow a person to live independently at home, such as meal preparation, driving, light

housework, managing finances, helping the person take medications, and arranging for medical care).

- Companionship services do not include domestic services performed mainly for the benefit of other members of the household. Companionship services do not include medically related services provided for the person.[58]

The new regulations also extend minimum wage and overtime coverage to companions employed by a third party employer, and extend overtime coverage to live-in domestic workers employed by a third party. The minimum wage and overtime exemptions for companions continue to apply to companions employed directly by individuals or families (provided the companions meet the new definition of companionship services). Live-in domestic workers employed directly by individuals or families continue to be exempt from overtime.

CHILD LABOR

The FLSA sets minimum age requirements for youth employed outside of school hours in agricultural and nonagricultural occupations. In non-agricultural occupations, the act sets a general minimum age for employment of 16. In agricultural occupations, the general minimum age to work is 14.[59]

The FLSA includes a number of exceptions to the general minimum age requirements of the act. Under a parental exemption, a child of any age may be employed by his or her parent (or person standing in the place of a parent) in any occupation in a business, including a farm, owned or operated by the parent. But, youth under 18 cannot be employed in mining or manufacturing, including in a business owned or operated by a parent.[60]

Youth under a certain age cannot work in occupations determined by the Secretary of Labor to be hazardous to minors. The minimum age to work in hazardous occupations in nonagricultural occupations is 18. In agricultural occupations, the minimum age is 16.

The FLSA also provides exemptions from the limits on employment in hazardous occupations. In agriculture, youth between the ages of 14 and 15 may work in certain hazardous occupations if they are student learners.[61] Minors ages 14 and 15 can operate tractors or other machinery if they hold a certificate of training from a 4-H or vocational agriculture training program.

The restrictions on employment in hazardous occupations in agriculture do not apply to youth employed on farms owned or operated by a parent.

Youth ages 12 and 13 can work in agriculture with the written consent of their parents on a farm where a parent (or person standing in the place of a parent) is also employed.

Youth who are covered by the FLSA and are not exempt must be paid at least the applicable federal or state minimum wage. However, employees in agriculture are exempt from the overtime requirements of the FLSA.[62]

On September 2, 2011, DOL issued a notice of proposed rulemaking (NPRM) to change the regulations that implement the child labor provisions in agriculture. In the proposed rule, DOL said that "None of the revisions proposed in this NPRM in any way change or diminish the statutory child labor parental exemption in agricultural employment" in the FLSA.[63] Nevertheless, in response to concerns about the potential effects of the proposed rule on the parental exemption, DOL announced, on February 1, 2012, that it was going to reconsider the part of the rule dealing with the interpretation of the parental exemption. DOL said that instead of applying the parental exemption to farms that are "wholly" owned by the parent (or person standing in place of a parent) the exemption would apply to farms that are "substantially" owned by the parent. Thus, the parental exemption would apply to farms where the parent is a part owner of the farm, a partner in a partnership, or an officer of a corporation that owns the farm if the parent holds a substantial ownership interest in the partnership or corporation.[64]

On April 26, 2012, DOL announced that it was withdrawing the proposed rule. DOL stated that "The decision to withdraw this rule—including provisions to define the 'parental exemption'— was made in response to thousands of comments expressing concerns about the effect of the proposed rules on small family-owned farms." DOL also stated that the regulation will not be pursued for the duration of the Obama Administration.[65]

Appendix. Major Amendments to the FLSA, Federal Minimum Wage Rates, and List of Acronyms

This appendix briefly describes major amendments to the Fair Labor Standards Act (FLSA). **Table A-1** shows the history of legislated changes in the basic federal minimum wage. **Table A-2** shows the minimum wage rates in the states and other jurisdictions as of January 1, 2012. **Table A-3** provides a list of acronyms used in the report.

Major Amendments to the FLSA

The FLSA has been amended several times since 1938.[66] The amendments generally expanded coverage of the act, created subminimum wage rates, and increased the basic minimum wage.

1947 Amendments

In 1947, Congress passed the Portal-to-Portal Act. The act addressed issues arising out of several court cases. First, Congress addressed the practical definition of hours worked, for which an employee must be paid. Congress excluded from hours worked time spent traveling to and from work. Congress also stated that some "preliminary" and "postliminary" activities performed before or after the workday are not hours worked.[67] However, workers could be compensated for such activities if the worker and employer agreed to such employment terms or if compensation for the activities was customary in the place of employment.[68]

The 1947 amendments also allow parties to settle a worker's minimum wage or overtime claim if "there exists a bona fide dispute as to the amount payable."[69] However, parties cannot agree to a settlement that would result in a wage less than the minimum wage or payment of less than time-and-a-half for overtime.[70]

Additionally, in the 1947 amendments Congress prohibited class action suits under the statute, unless the Secretary of Labor filed the suit as the representative of workers. It also limited the availability of compensation recovered in a class action suit only to those employees who affirmatively agreed to be a part of the suit.[71] Finally, the amendments set a two-year statute of limitation (time limit) in which a worker could file a claim.[72]

1961 and 1966 Amendments

In 1961, Congress amended FLSA exemptions such that employers of retail workers in enterprises with annual sales in excess of $1 million were required to pay minimum wage and overtime rates.[73]

In 1966, Congress expanded coverage of the FLSA to include workers employed in any enterprise with annual sales of at least $250,000 and employees of all businesses engaged in construction, repair, laundering, and cleaning services. Additionally, for the first time, FLSA coverage was extended to employees of hospitals, elementary and secondary schools, and institutions of higher education.[74] The 1966 amendments also added a "tip credit," which allowed employers to include a portion of an employee's tips as part of the minimum wage.[75] Finally, the 1966 amendments restricted the employment of youth under the age of 16 in agriculture in occupations found by the Secretary of Labor to be particularly hazardous, except when the employee is employed by a parent on a farm owned or operated by the parent.[76]

1974 Amendments

The 1974 FLSA amendments extended coverage to most federal, state, and local government employees. However, fire protection and law enforcement employees (including security personnel in correctional institutions) of public agencies were given special treatment, such as a complete exemption from overtime for agencies that employ fewer than five employees in fire protection or law enforcement and a partial exemption from overtime for fire protection and law enforcement employees whose work period extends from 7 to 28 consecutive days.[77]

1985 Amendments

In 1985, Congress amended the FLSA to allow state and local governments to offer their workers compensatory time off from work in lieu of overtime pay.[78]

1989 Amendments

In 1989, FLSA coverage was extended to enterprises with annual sales of at least $500,000. The amendments also repealed the retail exemption, under which employees of almost all small retail enterprises were exempt from the minimum wage and overtime rates.

The 1996 Small Business Job Protection Act

In 1996, Congress exempted certain computer professionals from minimum wage and overtime regulations.[79] The 1996 amendments also brought within the FLSA's minimum wage coverage all government employees employed as of April 1, 1996.

The 2007 Increases in the Basic Minimum Wage

On May 25, 2007, President George W. Bush signed into law a supplemental appropriations bill titled the "U.S. Troop Readiness, Veterans' Care, Katrina Recovery, and Iraq Accountability Appropriations Act, 2007" (P.L. 110-28). Title VIII of the act, "Fair Minimum Wage and Tax Relief," increased the basic federal minimum wage from $5.15 to $5.85 an hour effective July 2007, from $5.85 to $6.55 an hour effective July 2008, and from $6.55 to $7.25 an hour effective July 2009.

The Equal Pay Act

The Equal Pay Act (EPA), although commonly referred to on its own, was an amendment to the FLSA. The EPA was enacted in 1963 and prohibits gender-based pay discrimination.[80]

Break Time for Nursing Mothers

The 2010 Patient Protection and Affordable Care Act (PPACA) amended the FLSA to require covered employers to provide reasonable break time to nonexempt employees to express breast milk for a nursing child.

Table A-1. Federal Minimum Wage Laws

Public Law and Date Enacted	Wage Rate	Effective Date of Wage Rate
P.L. 75-718, enacted June 25, 1938	$0.25 0.30 0.40	October 1938 October 1939 October 1945
P.L. 81-393, enacted October 26, 1949	0.75	January 1950
P.L. 84-381, enacted August 12, 1955	1.00	March 1956
P.L. 87-30, enacted May 5, 1961	1.15 1.25	September 1961 September 1963
P.L. 89-601, enacted September 23, 1966	1.40 1.60	February 1967 February 1968
P.L. 93-259, enacted April 8, 1974	2.00 2.10 2.30	May 1974 January 1975 January 1976
P.L. 95-151, enacted November 1, 1977	2.65 2.90 3.10 3.35	January 1978 January 1979 January 1980 January 1981

Public Law and Date Enacted	Wage Rate	Effective Date of Wage Rate
P.L. 101-157, enacted November 17, 1989	3.80 4.25	April 1990 April 1991
P.L. 104-188, enacted August 20, 1996	4.75 5.15	October 1996 September 1997
P.L. 110-28, enacted May 25, 2007	5.85 6.55 7.25	July 2007 July 2008 July 2009

Source: CRS Report RL33791, *Possible Indexation of the Federal Minimum Wage: Evolution of Legislative Activity*, by William G. Whittaker.

Table A-2. Minimum Wage Rates in the States and Other Jurisdictions, as of January 1, 2014

Jurisdictions (22) With Minimum Wage Rates Higher Than the Federal Minimum Wage		
Alaska ($7.75)	Maine ($7.50)	New York ($8.00)
Arizona ($7.90)	Massachusetts ($8.00)	Ohio ($7.95)
California ($8.00)	Michigan ($7.40)	Oregon ($9.10)
Colorado ($8.00)	Missouri ($7.50)	Rhode Island ($8.00)
Connecticut ($8.70)	Montana ($7.90)	Vermont ($8.73)
District of Columbia ($8.25)	Nevada ($8.25)	Washington ($9.32)
Florida ($7.93)	New Jersey ($8.25)	
Illinois ($8.25)	New Mexico ($7.50)	
Jurisdictions (22) With Minimum Wage Rates the Same as the Federal Minimum Wage ($7.25)		
Delaware	Maryland	Texas
Guam	Nebraska	Utah
Hawaii	New Hampshire	U.S. Virgin Islands
Idaho	North Carolina	Virginia
Indiana	North Dakota	West Virginia
Iowa	Oklahoma	Wisconsin
Kansas	Pennsylvania	
Kentucky	South Dakota	
Jurisdictions (7) With Minimum Wage Rates Less Than the Federal Minimum Wage[a]		
American Samoa ($4.18-$5.59)[b]	Georgia ($5.15)	Puerto Rico ($5.08)
Arkansas ($6.25)	Minnesota ($6.15)	Wyoming ($5.15)

Table A-2. (Continued)

Commonwealth of the Northern Mariana Islands (CNMI) ($5.55)[c]		
Jurisdictions (5) With No State Minimum Wage Requirementa		
Alabama	Mississippi	Tennessee
Louisiana	South Carolina	

Source: U.S. Department of Labor, Wage and Hour Division, *Minimum Wage Laws in the States, January 1, 2014,* http://www.dol.gov/whd/minwage/america.htm.

Notes: Coverage patterns vary from one jurisdiction to another. The table shows the highest minimum wage applicable under current law.

[a] In states with a minimum wage that is lower than the federal minimum wage or with no minimum wage, state law applies to workers who are not covered by the FLSA.

[b] In American Samoa, the next wage increases are scheduled for September 30, 2015. The rates will then rise every three years until they reach the federal minimum wage. U.S. Department of Labor, Wage and Hour Division, *Federal Minimum Wage in American Samoa*, http://www.dol.gov/whd/minwage/americanSamoa/ASminwagePoster.pdf.

[c] The minimum wage in CNMI increased to $5.55 an hour on September 30, 2012. It is scheduled to rise to $6.05 an hour on September 30, 2014.

Table A-3. List of Acronyms

Acronym	Description
BLS	Bureau of Labor Statistics of the U.S. Department of Labor
CNMI	Commonwealth of the Northern Mariana Islands
DOL	U.S. Department of Labor
EAP	Executive, administrative, and professional employees
EPA	Equal Pay Act
FLSA	Fair Labor Standards Act
NIRA	National Industrial Recovery Act
NPRM	Notice of Proposed Rule Making
PPACA	Patient Protection and Affordable Care Act
SIC	Special Industrial Committees
SMW	Special minimum wage rates for persons with disabilities
SWEP	School Work Experience Program
WHD	Wage and Hour Division of the U.S. Department of Labor

End Notes

[1] Stephanie Fitzgerald, *The New Deal: Rebuilding America* (Minneapolis, MN: Compass Point Books, 2007), p. 77.

[2] This section of the report was written by Alexandra Hegji.

[3] **Table A-3** in the **Appendix** provides a list of acronyms used in the report.

[4] U.S. Congress, House of Representatives Committee on Labor, *Fair Labor Standards Act, Conference Report to Accompany S. 2475*, 75th Cong., 3rd sess., June 11, 1938, Report No. 2738, p. 28.

[5] U.S. Congress, Senate Committee on Education and Labor, *Fair Labor Standards Act, Report to Accompany S. 2475*,75th Cong., 1st sess., July 6, 1937, Report No. 884, p. 1.

[6] *Fair Labor Standards Act of 1938*, ch. 676, §§6, 7, and 12, 52 Stat. 1060, at 1062-64, 1067.

[7] Ibid.

[8] Although Congress articulated both social and economic reasons for regulating child labor, some commentators noted that President Roosevelt believed the addition of child labor provisions in the FLSA would make wage and hour provisions more palatable to Congress, thereby making FLSA enactment easier. Ibid.

[9] *Fair Labor Standards Act of 1938*, ch. 676, §§6, 7, 12, 52 Stat. 1060.

[10] Ibid., at 1067-1068.

[11] The size of an enterprise is measured by its "annual sales or business done." Annual sales or business done includes all business activities that can be measured in dollars. Thus, retailers are covered by the FLSA if their annual sales are at least $500,000. Owners of rental properties are covered if they collect at least $500,000 annually in rent. 29 C.F.R. §§779.258-779.259.

[12] U.S. Department of Labor, *Wages and Hours Worked: Minimum Wage and Overtime Pay*, available at http://www.dol.gov/compliance/guide/minwage.htm#who. 29 U.S.C. §203(s)(1).

[13] U.S. Department of Labor, *Coverage Under the Fair Labor Standards Act*, available at http://www.dol.gov/whd/regs/compliance/whdfs14.pdf. (Hereinafter cited as DOL, *Coverage Under the Fair Labor Standards Act.*)

[14] 29 U.S.C. §203(e).

[15] 29 U.S.C. §203(c).

[16] Other federal laws or regulations establish minimum wage requirements for workers. These rates are generally higher, but cannot be lower, than the applicable federal or state minimum wage. The Davis-Bacon Act requires employers to pay employees at least the locally prevailing wage and fringe benefits on construction contracts of more than $2,000 to which the federal government is a party. The Service Contract Act requires employers to pay workers at least the locally prevailing wage and fringe benefits on service contracts of more than $2,500 with the federal government. Unlike minimum wage rates under the FLSA, prevailing wages under the Davis-Bacon Act and Service Contract Act are not legislated by Congress. Rather, prevailing wages under the two acts are based on wage surveys conducted by or for the U.S. Department of Labor.

As required by the Immigration and Nationality Act (INA) or regulations, minimum wage requirements also apply to foreign workers entering the United States under certain permanent employment-based visas and temporary nonimmigrant visas (e.g., the H-1B visa for temporary professional workers, the H-2A visa for temporary agricultural workers, and the H-2B visa for temporary nonagricultural workers). The minimum wage requirements for these workers are generally based on wage surveys, collective bargaining agreements, or prevailing wages under the Davis-Bacon Act or Service Contract Act.

[17] See **Table A-1** in the **Appendix** for a history of federal laws that increased the basic minimum wage.

[18] See **Table A-2** in the **Appendix** for a list of state minimum wage rates.

[19] U.S. Department of Labor, Bureau of Labor Statistics, *Characteristics of Minimum Wage Workers: 2012*, February 26, 2013, http://www.bls.gov/cps/minwage2012.pdf, Table 1.

[20] 29 U.S.C. §203(m). In 1966, when the tip credit was added to the FLSA, an employer could claim up to 50% of the minimum wage as a tip credit. In 1996, the minimum cash wage for tipped employees was set at $2.13 an hour, which was 50% of the, then, minimum wage of $4.25 an hour.

[21] The five states that do not have minimum wage laws are Alabama, Louisiana, Mississippi, South Carolina, and Tennessee. In Georgia, tipped employees are exempt from the state minimum wage law. Puerto Rico allows a lower minimum wage for tipped workers than for nontipped workers.

[22] For a legislative history of Section 14(c), see out-of-print CRS Report RL30674, *Treatment of Workers with Disabilities Under Section 14(c) of the Fair Labor Standards Act*, by William G. Whittaker (available to congressional clients upon request).

[23] The certificates also allow the payment of wages that are less than the prevailing wages on contracts subject to the Service Contract Act (SCA).

[24] 29 C.F.R. §525.

[25] 29 U.S.C. §206(g).

[26] 29 C.F.R. §§520.201(c), 520.501(a), and 520.506(a).

[27] For more information on minimum wages in the territories, see CRS Report RL30235, *Minimum Wage in the Territories and Possessions of the United States: Application of the Fair Labor Standards Act*, by William G. Whittaker.

[28] The full name of P.L. 110-28 is the U.S. Troop Readiness, Veterans' Care, Katrina Recovery, and Iraq Accountability Appropriations Act, 2007.

[29] The title of the 2010 legislation is *To Clarify the Availability of Existing Funds for Political Status Education in the Territory of Guam, and for Other Purposes* (P.L. 111-244).

[30] U.S. Department of Labor, Wage and Hour Division, *Wage Rates in American Samoa*, http://www.dol.gov/whd/minwage/americanSamoa/ASminwage.htm.

[31] U.S. Department of Labor, Wage and Hour Division, *Federal Minimum Wage in the Commonwealth of the Northern Mariana Islands*, http://www.dol.gov/whd/regs/compliance/posters/cnmi.pdf.

[32] The title of the 2013 legislation is *To Amend P.L. 93-435 with Respect to the Northern Mariana Islands, Providing Parity with Guam, the Virgin Islands, and American Samoa* (P.L. 113-34).

[33] Some states have overtime laws that are more protective of employees than the FLSA; for example, overtime pay may be required if an employee works more than 8 or 12 hours in a day. See U.S. Department of Labor, Wage and Hour Division, *Wage and Hour Division (WHD) Minimum Wage Laws in the States, January 1, 2012*,http://www.dol.gov/whd/minwage/america.htm.

[34] For background on the legislative origins of Section 7(o), see CRS Report R43088, *Compensatory Time and the Working Families Flexibility Act of 2013*, by Benjamin Collins and Gerald Mayer.

[35] 29 C.F.R. §§553.20-553.28.

[36] Comp time for federal employees was first provided by the Federal Employees Pay Act of 1956 (P.L. 106) and is codified at Title 5 U.S.C. §5543.

[37] Section 7(r) of the FLSA was added by Section 4207, "Reasonable Break Time for Nursing Mothers," of PPACA.

[38] For more information on the exemption for executive, administrative, and professional employees, see CRS Report RL32088, *The Fair Labor Standards Act: A Historical Sketch of the Overtime Pay Requirements of Section 13(a)(1)*,by William G. Whittaker.

[39] Originally, the FLSA stated that regulations implementing the EAP exemption would be issued by the administrator of the newly created Wage and Hour Division (WHD) of DOL. The Fair Labor Standards Amendments of 1961 (P.L. 87-30) changed the authority to issue regulations from the administrator of the WHD to the Secretary of Labor.

[40] An employee whose total annual compensation is at least $100,000 is exempt if he or she "customarily and regularly" performs at least one of the job duties tests for executive, administrative, or professional employees. 29 C.F.R. §541.601.
Before 2004, under Section 13(a)(1), executive, administrative, or professional employees were exempt if they met either a long or a short test. Under both tests, to be exempt, an employee had to meet both a salary test and a job duties test. U.S. Department of Labor, Wage and Hour Division, "Defining and Delimiting the Terms 'Any Employee Employed in a Bona Fide Executive, Administrative, Professional, or Local Retailing Capacity, or in the Capacity of Outside Salesman,'" *Federal Register*, vol. 5, October 15, 1940, pp. 4077-4078.

[41] 29 C.F.R. §541.100.

[42] 29 C.F.R. §541.200.

[43] 29 C.F.R. §541.300.

[44] Obtaining orders for "the use of facilities" includes selling advertising time on radio, television, or in newspapers, and soliciting freight for railroads or other transportation companies. U.S. Department of Labor, Wage and Hour Division, *Exemption for Outside Sales Employees Under the Fair labor Standards Act (FLSA)*, http://www.dol.gov/whd/regs/compliance/fairpay/fs17f_outsidesales.pdf.

[45] 29 C.F.R. §541.500.

[46] *Christopher v. SmithKline Beecham Corp.*, No. 11-204, pp. 4-5, 14-15 (U.S. Supreme Court 2012).

[47] 29 C.F.R. §541.502.

[48] For more on the exemption for employees in computer-related occupations, see CRS Report R42141, *Computer-Related Occupations Under the Fair Labor Standards Act (FLSA)*, by Gerald Mayer.

[49] 29 C.F.R. §§541.302 (July 1, 1990, edition).

[50] U.S. Department of Labor, Wage and Hour Division, "Fair Labor Standards Act: Computer-Related Occupations; Exemption from Minimum Wage and Overtime Compensation Requirements; Final Rule," *Federal Register*, vol. 57, October 9, 1992, p. 46744.

[51] The minimum weekly salary of $455 may be paid in periods longer than a week (e.g., $910 biweekly or $1,971.66 a month). 29 C.F.R. §541.600(b).

[52] 29 C.F.R. §541.400(b).

[53] 29 C.F.R. §541.401.

[54] The 1974 amendments added Sections 6(f) and 7(l) to the FLSA. Section 6(f) extended minimum wage coverage to domestic service employees. Section 6(f) states that

> Any employee (1) who in any workweek is employed in domestic service in a household shall be paid wages at a rate not less than the wage rate in effect under subsection (b) of this section unless such employee's compensation for such service would not because of section 209(a)(6) of the Social Security Act (42 U.S.C. 409(a)(6)) constitute wages for the purposes of title II of such Act (42 U.S.C. 401 et seq.), [i.e., the employee's pay must be wages for purposes of Social Security] or (2) who in any workweek (A) is employed in domestic service in one or more households, and (B) is so employed for more than 8 hours in the aggregate, shall be paid wages for such employment in such workweek at a rate not less than the wage rate in effect under subsection (b) of this section. [Note: Section 6(b) requires employers to pay employees at least the minimum wage rate required in Section 6(a) of the FLSA.]

Section 7(l) extended overtime coverage to domestic service employees. Section 7(l) states that No employer shall employ any employee in domestic service in one or more households for a workweek longer than forty hours unless such employee receives compensation for such employment in accordance with subsection (a) of this section. [Note: Section 7(a) requires employers to pay covered employees at least one-and-a-half times their regular rate of pay for overtime.]

[55] DOL, *Coverage Under the Fair Labor Standards Act*.

[56] U.S. Department of Labor, Wage and Hour Division, "Application of the Fair Labor Standards Act to Domestic Service," Final rule, *Federal Register*, vol. 78, October 1, 2013, pp. 60454, 60556-60557. (Hereinafter cited as DOL, *Application of the Fair Labor Standards Act to Domestic Service.*)

[57] DOL, *Application of the Fair Labor Standards Act to Domestic Service,* p. 60457. A registered nurse may be exempt from the minimum wage and overtime standards of the FLSA as a professional employee under section 13(a)(1) of the act.

[58] DOL, *Application of the Fair Labor Standards Act to Domestic Service,* p. 60557.

[59] For more information on child labor, see CRS Report RL31501, *Child Labor in America: History, Policy, and Legislative Issues*, by Gerald Mayer.

[60] Information on the age limits for youth employment are from U. S. Department of Labor, Wage and Hour Division, *Child Labor Requirements in Agricultural Occupations Under the Fair Labor Standards Act*, Child Labor Bulletin 102,available at http://www.dol.gov/whd/regs/compliance/childlabor102.pdf; and U. S. Department of Labor, Wage and Hour Division, *Child Labor Provisions in Nonagricultural Occupations Under the Fair Labor Standards Act*, Child Labor Bulletin 101, available at http://www.dol.gov/whd/regs/compliance/childlabor101.pdf.

[61] A student learner is someone who is enrolled in a vocational education program in agriculture under a written agreement that, among other things, ensures that the work of the student is incidental to the training.

[62] 29 U.S.C. 213(b)(12). Employees on small farms are exempt from both the minimum wage and overtime requirements of the FLSA. A farmer who did not employ more than 500 "man days" of labor in any calendar quarter in the preceding calendar year is exempt from the minimum wage and overtime requirements of the act. A "man day" is any day in which an employee performed agricultural work for at least one hour.

[63] U.S. Department of Labor, Wage and Hour Division, "Child Labor Regulations, Orders and Statements of Interpretation; Child Labor Violations—Civil Money Penalties," *Federal Register*, vol. 76, September 2, 2011, available at http://www.gpo.gov/fdsys/pkg/FR-2011-09-02/pdf/2011-21924.pdf, p. 54841.

[64] U.S. Department of Labor, Wage and Hour Division, *U.S. Labor Department to Re-Propose 'Parental Exemption' of Child Labor in Agriculture Rule*, February 1, 2012, http://www.dol.gov/opa/media/press/whd/WHD20120203.htm.

[65] U.S. Department of Labor, Wage and Hour Division, *Labor Department Statement on Withdrawal of Proposed Rule Dealing With Children Who Work in Agricultural Vocations,* http://www.dol.gov/opa/media/press/whd/ WHD20120826.htm.

[66] The review of major amendments to the FLSA was written by Alexandra Hegji.

[67] For instance, absent an employer-worker agreement or workplace custom, employers may not be required to pay workers minimum wage or overtime pay for the time workers spend changing clothes at the beginning and end of shifts while on work premises. See, for example, *Genuth v. National Biscuit Co.*, 81 F. Supp. 213 (S.D.N.Y. 1948).

[68] 29 U.S.C. §252.

[69] 29 U.S.C. §253(a).

[70] Ibid.

[71] 29 U.S.C. §216.

[72] 29 U.S.C. §255.

[73] *Fair Labor Standards Amendments of 1961*, P.L. 87-30.

[74] 1966 U.S.C.C.A.N. §3003, 3008.

[75] 29 U.S.C. §203(m).

[76] U.S. House of Representatives, *Fair Labor Standards Amendments of 1966, Conference Report to Accompany H.R. 13712*, 89th Cong., 2nd sess., Report No. 2004, September 6, 1966, p. 18.

[77] *Fair Labor Standards Amendments*, 1974, P.L. 93-259.

[78] *Fair Labor Standards Amendments of 1985*, P.L. 99-150.

[79] 29 U.S.C. §213(a)(17).
[80] 29 U.S.C. §§206-209.

INDEX

A

B

C

D

E

F

G

H

I

J

L

M

N

O

P

R

S